Windsor
CHAIRMAKING

Windsor
CHAIRMAKING

JAMES MURSELL

THE CROWOOD PRESS

First published in 2009 by
The Crowood Press Ltd
Ramsbury, Marlborough
Wiltshire SN8 2HR

www.crowood.com

British Library Cataloguing-in-Publication Data
A catalogue record for this book is available from the British Library.

ISBN 978 1 84797 154 8

Dedication
To Louise

Typeset by Sharon Kemmett/Isis Design
Printed and bound in Malaysia by Konway Printhouse Sdn Bhd

CONTENTS

INTRODUCTION

The golden period for Windsor chairs was between 1720 and 1800, just eighty years, or one lifetime. It is tempting for contemporary Windsor enthusiasts to wish to have been born during this exciting period, but we are probably much luckier to be alive today. We are able to see examples of the whole spectrum of chairs that were produced in this period from the distance of over two centuries, in spite of the loss and destruction of the vast majority of old chairs.

Most makers in the mid-eighteenth century would have been exposed to only a limited range of furniture, and most of that would have been made locally and exhibited only minor variation. Development was mainly incremental, but every now and again a step change would have been made by enterprising and imaginative makers who had been exposed to a much greater variety of influences, perhaps in London.

We must thank those early innovators who took the simple concept of a Windsor chair and developed it into a worldwide phenomenon, starting with individual makers and leading into the industrial production in the nineteenth century that epitomized the Victorian Industrial Revolution.

Today, with relatively inexpensive travel and the internet, we can study furniture from all over the world, and in particular Windsors from England and America. We are also fortunate that dedicated scholars have researched so thoroughly the developments of Windsor chairmaking on both sides of the Atlantic, in particular Nancy Goyne Evans who has produced the seminal works on the origins of Windsors and the development of American Windsor chairs, and Dr Bernard 'Bill' Cotton who has studied nineteenth-century English chairs so thoroughly.

Although interest in Windsor chairs almost died out in England and America at the beginning of the twentieth century, there has been a major revival in the past thirty years. Michael Harding-Hill and Charles Santore have championed the merits of eighteenth-century Windsors in England and America respectively, while Mike Dunbar and Jack Hill have introduced thousands of people to the delights of the chairs through their teaching.

Windsor chairs are still made today using industrial techniques. The best known manufacturer in Britain is probably Ercol, and many people who bought chairs from that com-

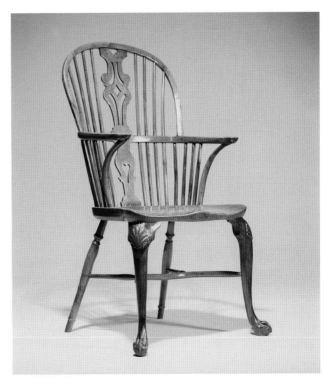

**English double-bow in yew fruitwood and elm.
(Courtesy Michael Harding-Hill)**

pany in the sixties are still proud owners, and keenly aware of the link to the past that these chairs represent. Windsors seem to be firmly embedded, even today, as a significant element in the histories of both England and America. Sadly many modern Windsors are not of such high quality as Ercol chairs. English pubs are full of modern manufactured Windsors, which aesthetically are quite depressing to anyone with an appreciation for the originals; and in America also, industrially produced Windsors can be seen everywhere. Unexciting as their designs may be, at least Windsors are still being made and used in good numbers.

This book will concentrate on chairs from that 'golden' period prior to 1800, and will pay little attention to chairs and designs made after that time. This reflects the author's interests and inclinations, and should not discourage further study of these later chairs.

Windsor chairs, even though they may have started life in the cities of London and Philadelphia, are nowadays considered 'country' furniture, and occupy a place in the woodworking pantheon with ladderback chairs. Both can be made with just the simplest of hand tools, and do not require the mastery

Checking the cut end of a felled oak tree for shakes – no problems were found.

A modern industrially made double-bow chair by Ercol. (Courtesy Ercol)

of specialist techniques such as the cutting of dovetail joints before the first Windsor or ladderback is made. Thus the world of country chairs is far more accessible to woodworkers and prospective woodworkers than most forms of furniture. This is somewhat paradoxical as cabinet makers often consider chairs to be amongst the most difficult items to make. This relatively simple form of construction allowed artisans from other fields, such as wheelwrights, to make Windsors as part of their output as far back as the 1750s, and it is a good reason, for anybody who is interested, to make a chair today. It is hoped that this book will encourage the process.

The fact that green wood can be used for the chair's construction is another feature that makes them attractive to people in the modern world. John Alexander in America and Mike Abbott in the UK have done more than most to publicize and promote green woodworking. Their enthusiasm for this type of material coincided with our increasing awareness of the environment and the importance of a sustainable lifestyle,

Gimson ladderback chair with rush seat 1892 – 1904.
(© Victoria and Albert Museum, London)

Ladderback chair by Brian Boggs.
(Courtesy Brian Boggs)

both globally and individually. The use of the same word 'green' to describe both fresh, wet wood and also 'consideration for the environment' only enhances the interest that exists today for Windsor chairs, whether making new chairs or collecting/studying old chairs.

It is probably worth another word about ladderback chairs. Although they have a longer history than Windsors, they have never achieved quite the same prominence. Probably the best known examples were made by the highly commercial Shakers in America, who in the nineteenth century developed and promoted their chairs to make money for their communities. In England more recently the chairs of Gimpson and others have had a great following. Nobody can deny these chairs' undoubted elegance, but it is perhaps possible to question their comfort in some cases. The reason for this is that ladderbacks tend to make fewer concessions to the human frame

than Windsors – backs tend to be more vertical, and seats are not moulded to fit the posterior of sitters. However, some current makers, such as Brian Boggs, have combined form and function so successfully that comfort ceases to be an issue.

It may already be obvious that 'country' chairmakers tend to fall into either the 'ladderback' or 'Windsor' camp, but not both. It is a little like the love of cats and dogs, where most people love one or the other, but seldom both, though there are exceptions. Dave Sawyer, who makes the finest Windsors that I am aware of, in the woods of northern Vermont, began by making ladderbacks, but progressed to Windsors. He describes the Windsor as the Stradivarius of chairs, and I agree wholeheartedly with this sentiment!

There is little doubt that Windsor chairs can become an addiction. You need only look at the number of people who have devoted significant parts of their lives to their study and making. No doubt each person is attracted to different aspects of these chairs, but I will try to explain what caused the addiction in me.

When I was very young my parents had Windsor chairs around our dining-room table, but soon acquired a set of Chippendale-style chairs from my grandmother. These were elegant chairs, but had embroidered seats stuffed with horse hair, which was none too comfortable on the legs to a young lad in short trousers. One up to Windsors!

At this same young age my father taught me to appreciate the pleasures of making things of wood, and this, combined with the love of these simple chairs, lodged in the back of my mind and lay dormant for almost thirty years. In the meantime I followed an academic rather than a practical education, culminating in a degree in botany. An MBA led to a number of years working in industry, both in England and America, and although I didn't appreciate it at the time, this period of living in America would be a major influence in my chairmaking career.

In the mid-eighties I took over part of the family fruit-growing business, and after several years began, in the winter evenings, to make simple furniture based on lessons learned from my father and at school. Nearly thirty years had passed since I had sat on those Windsor chairs of my youth, but taking a chairmaking course to develop hand skills rekindled this interest and ignited a passion that has never left.

It was the simplicity of construction, and the ease with which one could create a thing of beauty and utility, that grabbed my attention. This combination perfectly matched the way that I work and think, and has informed my chairmaking ever since.

To bring my story up to date, chairmaking began to dominate my leisure time. I began to make chairs as a hobby, and within two years had taken a second course, this time in America. This introduced me to green woodworking, and finally gave me the means to begin creating the chairs that I could picture in my head. Sadly, fruit growing was becoming unviable and I closed down my farm in 2001. The upside of this difficult decision, and one that I have never regretted, is that it allowed me to devote all my time to Windsor chairs.

Ten days of formal instruction and fifteen years of self-apprenticeship have brought me to where I am now – and I'm still learning!

Windsor chairs are far more sculptural and organic in form than most cabinet work, and this is due to the lack of flat surfaces, parallel lines or right-angles. In addition, when sympa-

thetically made, they combine the very best of form and function. The scope for experiment and development is also almost infinite. What more could one ask for as a woodworker?

Comparing cabinet making to Windsor chairmaking is like comparing apples and oranges. If cabinet making is 90 per cent about making joints and 10 per cent about shaping wood, then Windsor chairmaking is the opposite – 90 per cent shaping and 10 per cent joints.

Chairs can be made by an individual, or they can be produced by machines in factories with minimal human intervention, and with every combination of man and machine in between.

It is interesting to consider at what point the 'quality' of a machine-made chair will be surpassed by a hand-made chair.

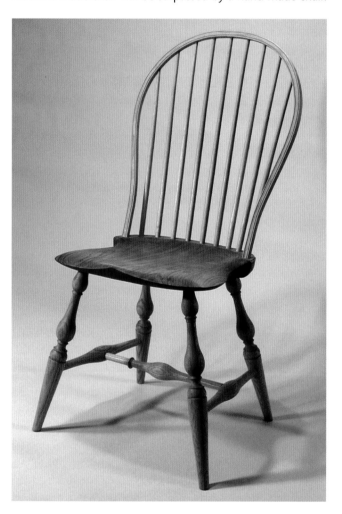

Balloon-back Windsor chair by Dave Sawyer.
(Courtesy Dave Sawyer)

However, 'quality' when applied to chairs is a characteristic that is hard to pin down, but it includes such things as structural soundness of joints, success of the shape of individual components and the whole, and the finish. The first priority of a chair is that it will perform its function of supporting a body without breaking, and do so over many years. Once that has been achieved, and this depends on the quality of the joints, then the chair can be judged on the aesthetic features of shape and finish. If you agree that Windsor chairmaking is '10 per cent joints and 90 per cent shaping', then this points the way to success for an individual maker.

When one starts making Windsor chairs for the first time, the challenge is to complete the chair with as few mistakes as possible. There are so many steps in the process that mistakes are almost inevitable, but eventually the process will become instinctive. Until these mistakes are eliminated in the handmade chairs, the good quality machine-made chair may be considered superior.

The quality of the machine-made chair will depend on the original design, the tolerances of production and, to a small extent, the skill of the person assembling the final chair. It is inevitable that it will be the product of economic compromises which will lead to a chair that is shaped to the economic rather than the aesthetic optimum. The individual maker has the time and opportunity to aim for aesthetic perfection. In fact he must strive for it, as this is all that sets his work apart from the mass or batch produced competition!

This book will cover most aspects of Windsor chairmaking, but with the overriding ambition of encouraging the making of chairs that are both structurally sound and elegant.

The Structure of this Book

I have written this book with readers of widely different experience in mind, and am sure that it will be used in many different ways. It is a distillation of all that is important to me about Windsor chairs, covering far more that just 'how to make a chair'. With this in mind, I offer a brief description of each chapter so that you can pick out those that are of most immediate interest – though I do not wish to put anyone off from the traditional approach of reading from start to finish!

Chapter 1	Starting with a definition, this chapter gives a brief description of how Windsor chairs have evolved historically and in design, both in England and America.
Chapter 2	The ingredients needed to make a Windsor chair. Traditional and non-traditional materials are considered. The ideal tools and equipment are detailed, along with a list giving the minimum requirements.
Chapter 3	How to make chairs. This covers techniques for each stage of chair making. Pick and choose depending on the project in hand. There is a great emphasis on the use of hand tools.
Chapter 4	Plans and specifications for two English Windsor chairs.
Chapter 5	Plans and specifications for two American Windsor chairs.
Chapter 6	Looks in detail at a magnificent English armchair made in the mid-1700s. Lessons are drawn from the extensive tool marks that the maker left on the chair. Finally the philosophy of the maker is discussed with implications for current makers.
Chapter 7	How do the relative angles and shapes of a chair's components affect how we see it? The body language of chairs is discussed, and guidance is given towards designing your own original chair.
Chapter 8	Moving beyond side and armchairs, much more can be made using the same techniques described in the rest of the book.

CHAPTER 1

HISTORY

What is a Windsor Chair?

A Windsor chair has a solid wooden seat into which pieces are socketed from below and above, to create legs and backs respectively. There is no connection between the elements above and below the seat other than through the seat itself. This somewhat formal definition describes a form of construction rather than a style, and many people are disappointed that their mental picture of what a Windsor chair should look like is but one example, rather than definitive. The presence of spindles (or sticks) in the back, a steam-bent bow or a pierced splat does not make a Windsor chair, though they may well form part of one.

Once you absorb the definition, it becomes liberating, and the possibilities of this form of construction become clearer. Chairs are not the only items that can be made in this way, although they are by far and away the most common. In Chapter 8 I briefly explore a few other types of furniture that can be made using the same techniques. The use of this form of construction is restricted only by imagination, and by the number of people familiar with its use and who are prepared to solve woodworking problems in this way, rather than using a more 'conventional' approach.

A Windsor chair has a solid wooden seat. The other components are socketed into the seat from above and below, but with no direct connnection between them.

Early Windsor Chairs and Stools

The ancient Egyptians made stools using the Windsor method around 3,000 years ago, so it is hardly new! Once boring tools had been developed, people must have inserted sticks into planks. Three sticks of equal length and equally spaced inserted into a plank make a 'milking' stool, which is stable on all surfaces. The Egyptian stools varied in height: sometimes the legs were straight, and at other times curved; also the seats varied in thickness, and in some cases were dished to make them more comfortable. Even with these few variables the style of stool that is possible is enormous. The Egyptians had also learned to turn wood, so they possessed all the technology needed to make Windsor chairs – though as far as we know they did not convert their stools into chairs!

The first picture of a chair that we would recognize today as a Windsor was painted in Botticelli's studio in 1483 in Florence. This chair has a thick 'D'-shaped seat supported by three tapered (square-section) legs, with two in the front and one at the back. The superstructure features a 'U'-shaped arm (following the shape of the back of the seat) mounted on eight turned spindles. This is the one of the first pictures known to show socketing of elements into the top surface of the seat. This idea obviously did not catch on in Italy at the time, and it had to wait more than 200 years before it became popular in England.

Most early 'Windsor' chairs and stools did not have stretchers, and the individual legs were held in place solely by the mortice and tenon joint in the seat. This necessitated a thick seat and substantial tenons to give a sufficiently strong joint. The first record of stretchers in 'Windsor' furniture is a Dutch painting from 1661, which shows a round stool with three well splayed legs joined together with three stretchers. It is surprising that this practice did not evolve earlier, as purely turned furniture depended absolutely on horizontal members holding the vertical pieces together.

The restoration of the monarchy in England in 1660 marked the transition from joined, mainly oak seating to the turned and carved styles that Charles II brought back with him from

Restoration chair, 1685–1693. Carved and turned walnut, with caned panels. (© Victoria and Albert Museum, London)

the Continent. In the broadest sense it seems that joiners tended towards cabinet making, while seating became the province of the turner/chairmakers. After the Restoration, heavily carved, caned chairs became the height of fashion, and it was only when these began to fall from favour in the early 1700s that turner/chairmakers began to make Windsor chairs instead.

The first reference to a Windsor seat was in 1718, describing seating found in the garden of Dyrham Park near Bath. However, it appears that this was not of the form that we know today as Windsor, but referred to seats made of planks that could be rotated in order to shelter from the wind and sun. Nevertheless, the association with formal gardens was crucial to the development of the early Windsors as we know them, because these may have been a forerunner to the 'modern' Windsor in the form of Forest chairs, which began to appear around 1710. These were made of branch wood with the bark retained, and it was a small step to them being made of turned wood, giving rise to our understanding of Windsor chairs.

It is suggested by Goyne Evans that the link with 'Windsor' came from such chairs being seen in the grounds of Windsor Castle. Nobody knows for sure how the name came about, but there is no evidence that they were made in the town itself; it may even be true that the earliest chairs were made in London, where most of the recorded turners worked. This is supported in part by the earliest known advertisement for Windsor chairs in a newspaper dated 1730. John Brown advertised 'All sorts of Windsor garden chairs, of all sizes, painted green or in the wood'. His workshop was in St Paul's Churchyard, London.

Whatever the truth about the origins of the name 'Windsor' as applied to chairs, there are other examples of where a product has acquired its name from a location where it was never made. Stilton cheese is named after a town in Cambridgeshire, England, where it was first sold at a pub that lay on the Great North Road. The cheese originated near Melton Mowbray, Leicestershire, and was never made in Stilton itself, but acquired its name though the marketing of the product. A second example is the Panama hat: these hats are all made in Ecuador, but acquired their current name when the Panama Canal was being built. Many of the workers wore this type of hat, and the name was subsequently adopted. Again, the product was never made in the place that it was named after.

Early Use and Styles

Once the chairs acquired the comb-back form that we are now familiar with, they became essential furniture for the aristocracy's formal gardens. They were almost all painted green to blend into the garden setting and presumably to protect them from the elements. The chairs did not remain solely in the garden for long; on his death in 1736, Lord Byron's house (Newstead Abbey, Nottinghamshire) contained the following Windsor furniture indoors:

RED GALLERY	4 double Windsors
GREAT GALLERY	4 trebles and 6 singles
LITTLE GALLERY	4 Windsors
BLUE GALLERY	1 treble and 1 single

It was their adoption and endorsement by the aristocracy that set Windsor chairs off on such a dizzying trajectory over the next 150 years. The patronage of rich and powerful owners made the chairs desirable to those that sought to emulate their 'betters', but the secret of the Windsor chair's success lay in the way that it was made. The sensitive shaping of the chairs leads one to the conclusion that in the early days each chair was made by one craftsman, perhaps with the assistance of apprentices. But it was the ability to make each part of the chair in large numbers, and then to assemble chairs from a stock of parts, that generated economies of scale and the possibility of a significant reduction in the price. This process did not happen all at once, but chair factories – the embodiment of economies of scale – were in existence by the 1790s.

In the early eighteenth century the price of Windsors was on a scale between rush-seated chairs and cabinet makers' chairs, being roughly double the cost of the former and half the price of the latter. This pricing position, along with the comfort of a sculpted seat, and their initial unique position as outdoor chairs, meant that they filled a niche in the market. Were these chairs deliberately created by entrepreneurs to fill this niche, rather than evolving by chance? It is unlikely that we will ever know, given how thin the historical record is. All that can be said is that most of the evolution took place in the first eighty years of their existence, after which the basic chair patterns were recycled and modified.

Manufacturing Evolution

The study of the evolution of Windsor chairs from the historical record is fraught with the same challenges as the study of biological evolution from the fossil record. In both cases many gaps exist, and transitional forms are very rare. Another common feature is that a period of explosive evolution was followed by relative stability and lack of innovation.

The price of Windsors was first brought down by a division of labour to create the components. Relatively low-skilled individuals became specialists in creating different parts for the chairs, and so each part was made with the greatest possible efficiency. With this specialization the parts became virtually commodity items, with the associated loss of value. In America the Philadelphia chairmaker Trumble advertised for 40,000 hand-shaved hickory spindles in 1775. Anyone who has

shaved their own spindles can appreciate the amount of work involved. Assuming five minutes per spindle, including time for splitting the blanks, this translates to 3,333 hours, or eighty-three weeks of forty hours doing nothing else, for one man! Bodgers working in the woods above High Wycombe in the nineteenth century were not paid highly for their production, and the relationship between them and the factories must have been similar to today's suppliers to supermarkets.

As the Industrial Revolution progressed, machinery played an increasingly important role, gradually replacing the human inputs and reducing costs still further. As these developments progressed, the decline in the aesthetic qualities of the chairs can be seen: in England they tended to became heavier, while in America the simpler designs relied increasingly on paint and decoration to make them attractive.

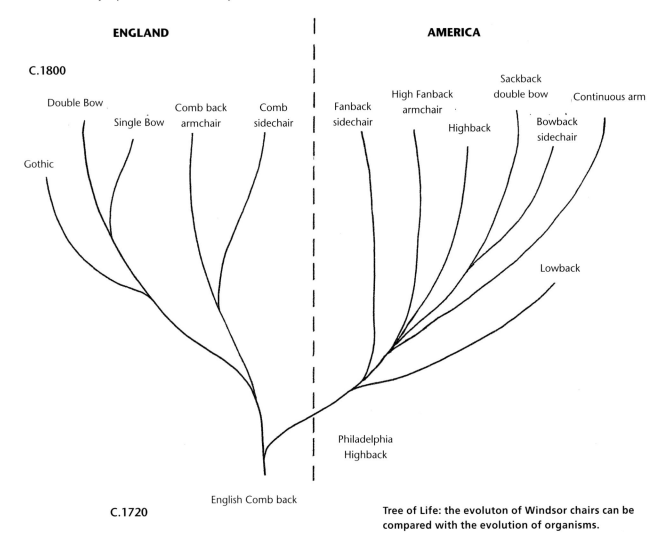

ENGLAND

C.1800

Double Bow

Single Bow

Comb back armchair

Comb sidechair

Gothic

English Comb back

C.1720

AMERICA

Fanback sidechair

High Fanback armchair

Sackback double bow

Continuous arm

Highback

Bowback sidechair

Lowback

Philadelphia Highback

Tree of Life: the evoluton of Windsor chairs can be compared with the evolution of organisms.

It is very difficult to create the same quality of chair when it is made by many people from stock parts, compared with a chair made by an individual; but the unfortunate reality for today's makers is that these less expensive chairs perform the task of supporting a human body almost as well as the hand-made version. So although comfort and aesthetic quality may be compromised, they may nevertheless be quite sufficient for most of the market.

The first Windsors, as we now know them, were developed in England. They had 'D'-shaped seats, steam-bent arms, and long spindles topped with a crest to form the back. In front of these long spindles the arm was supported by short spindles. Many of the earliest chairs did not have stretchers between the legs.

Windsor Chairs in America

These chairs were not confined to England for long. They had crossed the Atlantic to Philadelphia before 1736, when the will of Patrick Gordon (Governor of Pennsylvania) included mention of Windsor chairs. It is thought that production of domestic chairs did not begin in Philadelphia until around 1740, but the first chairs bore a striking resemblance to their English cousins. The most obvious characteristics that distinguished them from their forebears were the adoption of different turning patterns, and an increased splay to the legs. The latter characteristic continued to distinguish American from English chairs throughout their histories (*see* Chapter 7). Shortly after the production of these high-back chairs began, low-back versions were also developed. The seat, arm-posts and undercarriage remained virtually unchanged, but the steam-bent bow was replaced with a three-piece 'sawn' arm, supported along

Very early English Windsor comb-back, 1700–1750. Elm seat, sticks and arm-bow of ash, oak legs, all painted green. (© Victoria and Albert Museum, London)

Philadelphia high-back. (Courtesy Charles Santore)

its length by short spindles.

Around 1750 in England, cabriole legs and baluster splats were incorporated into Windsor chairs. These embellishments were taken from earlier cabinet makers' chairs and would have increased the cost of production considerably. By now the chairs were undoubtedly used mainly indoors, but the market had broadened from the aristocracy to the professional and merchant classes. While the market developed in a similar way in America, these new features were not adopted. The splat became almost de rigueur in English chairs from that time onwards, though the use of cabriole legs declined. These expensive legs were not consistent with the constant push to reduce prices and expand the market.

It was in this period that John Pitt (1714–1759) from Slough, near Windsor, made the chair that is considered to be the oldest provenanced Windsor chair. The distinctively carved cabriole legs set his chairs apart from others of the same period, but have allowed several other chairs to be attributed to him over the past ten years.

The next development in England at a similar time was that of the double-bow chair. The crest was substituted for a sec-ond steam-bent bow that was tenoned into the arm, and into which the tops of the spindles were fitted. It was common in these c. 1750 English chairs for the crests to be supported on spindles and a ribbon slat at either end. These rectangular cross-sectioned pieces were also incorporated in the first double bows, but this practice was quickly dropped – presumably because it was unnecessary, and added to the complication and cost.

The double bow was adopted in Philadelphia in the 1760s, but by now the styles on each side of the Atlantic were quite distinct, the American chairs having become generally lighter in appearance than the English. Although it is dangerous to generalize, it is my opinion that it is the spaces between components that dominate in American chairs, while in English chairs it is the components themselves that catch the eye. In England there was a brief fashion for gothic-style chairs, distinguished by their pointed backs, though occasionally produced with round backs, and with all spindles replaced by pierced splats.

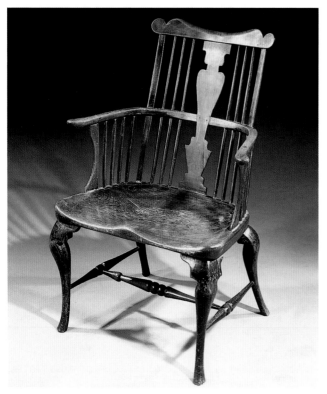

The 'Pitt' chair. (© Christie's Images Limited)

English armchair in elm yew and fruitwood. The four cabriole legs, crinoline stretcher, ribbon slats and fretted splat make this an impressive chair. (Courtesy Michael Harding-Hill)

American double-bow chair. (Courtesy Charles Santore)

**Continuous-arm chair from New York.
(Courtesy Winterthur Museum)**

As we move towards the end of the eighteenth century almost all splats in English chairs became pierced, and makers incorporated many contemporary patterns in them. The most commonly known pattern that uses the pierced wheel as its dominant motif became popular at the end of the century, and has been used continuously up to the present day. Ask most people today in Britain to picture a Windsor chair, and they would probably describe a 'wheelback' chair.

In America Windsor chairmaking spread from Philadelphia to New York, Boston and Rhode Island, and to country areas around these centres. The most dramatic development, which was entirely American, was the creation of the continuous armchair in New York City in around 1790. The single piece, steam-bent bow tied all the spindles together to create the flowing shape of the Bergère chair that may have been the inspiration.

The first side chairs, as opposed to armchairs, in England and Philadelphia were fanbacks, following the same pattern of development as the armchairs, and were made in the 1750s. The backs of these English chairs were usually made up of a splat, spindles and two outer ribbon slats, all joined together with a horizontal crest. Frequently the back would have been braced with two extra spindles inserted into a projection behind the seat. The legs of the earlier chairs may have been in the cabriole style, but they became uniformly turned as time went on.

In Philadelphia elegant fanbacks were made by Henzey and Trumble in the 1770s, developing their designs from the earlier prototypes. These later chairs had turned back-posts and spindles that supported a fine crest. Bow-back chairs developed around 1770 in both countries, though they gained prominence in America prior to England.

The shape of seats changed over time in both countries. In England the 'D'-shaped seat quickly became more rectangular and developed a swell around the front legs, while in America the initial 'D'-shaped seat evolved first into the oval and then the shield shape. Both oval and shield patterns have been used continuously to the present day.

Given the simplicity of their form of construction, and the huge success that they enjoyed in Britain and America both in their domestic markets and as exports, it is very strange that they only appear to have been successful in English-speaking countries. Goyne Evans identifies the Sgabello chairs that developed in northern Italy prior to the earliest Windsors. Although they comply with the definition of a Windsor chair, their flat plank seats and backs bear little resemblance to the chairs that we would describe as Windsor.

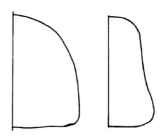

Development of seat shape – England.

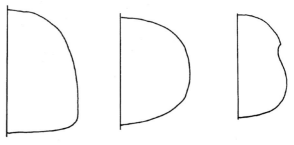

Development of seat shape – America ('D' shape to Oval to Shield).

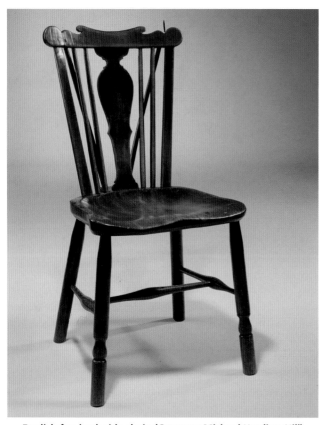

English fan-back side chair. (Courtesy Michael Harding-Hill)

American fan-back side chair. (Courtesy Nancy Goyne-Evans)

Production of Windsors Today

The last chairmaking factories in High Wycombe closed down in the twentieth century, but it is remarkable how frequently I still meet people who can remember going into the woods above the town and seeing the bodgers at work. There is little doubt that these bodgers would have been the last of their kind, but they are still remembered with interest, and as part of our cultural history. This collective memory may well be due to great publicity generated by chairmaking businesses, but must also be due to research and recording by organizations such as the Shell Film Unit that produced a number of excellent black and white films, recording the life of the bodgers.

Their life must have been very hard, having to work in all weathers with little protection. This lifestyle has been re-enacted by pole-lathers all around the UK, and proves to be very popular, particularly during the summer months.

Today the private ownership of Windsor chairs is treated differently in Britain and America. In Britain the market for quality hand-made Windsors is small, and is limited to those who appreciate and can afford fine furniture. However, a number of businesses continue to survive making good quality reproductions produced in a semi-industrial way. In America, by contrast, Windsor chairs can be described as aspirational furniture. You need only watch Hollywood blockbusters carefully and you will see one or more Windsor chairs in most films. By contrast British films virtually never include them, except in period dramas; there was just one in the whole series of the Harry Potter films, and that was in deep shade!

The value ascribed to Windsor chairs on either side of the Atlantic is another measure of their popularity. The largest ever bid at auction in Britain is around £20,000, while in America chairs have been known occasionally to change hands for $500,000.

The ongoing tradition of painting Windsors in America is something that finds little resonance in Britain. All Windsors were painted in the early 1700s, but this ceased in England as the chairs were brought indoors. Many theories exist about why the practice continues in America, but not in England. Perhaps American homes tended to have more exposed wood in the living rooms, and the colour of painted chairs livened up the overall appearance. Another explanation is that the chairs are always made of several different woods, and American seat wood (pine or tulip) is not particularly attractive, so painting the whole chair unifies the whole piece, and adds colour to its surroundings. By contrast English chairs always used elm for the seats, and some of the other woods, particu-

Painted Windsor chair. (Courtesy Winterthur Museum)

larly yew, are very attractive in their own right – hence no need to paint over them.

Whatever the reasons, painting is just one feature that distinguishes American chairs from English, along with a lightness of construction and a rake and splay of components that seem exaggerated to British eyes.

Each person must decide on which tradition to follow. It is difficult to work in both styles at the same time as there are so many nuances that differ and which, if not observed, will jar the eye of anyone knowledgeable. My hope is that this book will encourage new people to begin making Windsors, and that existing makers may pick up some tips, and perhaps also try their hand at making chairs from the opposite side of the Atlantic.

CHAPTER 2

MATERIALS, EQUIPMENT AND TOOLS

Wood

The definition of Windsor furniture involves a form of construction limited to one material – wood. It is possible to imagine metal or plastic Windsor chairs, but the nature of these materials means that there are much better ways of joining parts together than the mortice and tenon joints that are ubiquitous in Windsor furniture. Metal is more likely to be welded, while plastic is usually glued or welded, or moulded into a single piece. One cannot say that metal is never used, but the occasional situations in which it was used in old chairs almost always involved attaching the arm to a back-post or arm-post.

Although Windsor chairs have solid wooden seats by definition, some were designed to be upholstered, with fabric added on top of the seat. In this situation the makers made little effort to shape the seat, relying on the padding to provide comfort, rather than the careful shaping of the solid seat. Fortunately limiting yourself to wood as the sole material is not too restricting. Each species has its own distinct combina-

tion of hardness, colour, grain pattern, strength, density and so on; and with hundreds of species to choose from, you will be spoilt for choice. The down side of this variation is that there is never a single wood that will be ideal for each role. A metal or plastic chair can be made using the same material throughout, but you are unlikely ever to find an old Windsor chair made of a single species of wood.

The woods that were chosen for chairmaking 200 years ago were inevitably grown locally. We have become so used to wood being imported from all around the world that the link between furniture and locally grown species has largely been lost. This is a trend that is beginning to reverse, however, with the greater awareness of the true costs of transport. Also, it must be said, there is something attractive about making a product with local origins. Sadly it is not easy, though not impossible, to produce a Windsor chair made entirely of locally grown wood. It is a worthy ambition to minimize the use of wood imported from outside one's local area, and it can make a key selling-point when marketing your work.

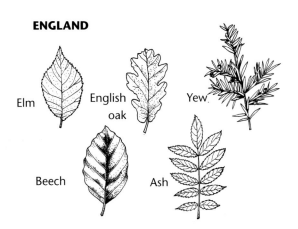

ENGLAND

Elm

English oak

Yew

Beech

Ash

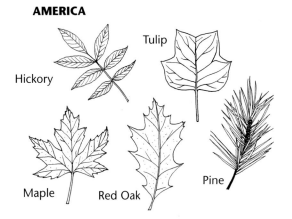

AMERICA

Hickory

Tulip

Maple

Red Oak

Pine

England: Traditional Woods

WOODS FOR SEATS

The one constant feature of antique English Windsor chairs is the choice of elm for the seat. Every other feature varies, but the seat wood stays the same. Why is this? The elm, prior to Dutch elm disease, was our largest native tree, found all over England, and particularly in hedgerows. The wood was not highly prized for furniture, house building or ship construction, and was therefore less expensive than other large-girthed trees such as oak. Elm was used for coffins, weatherboarding on the sides of buildings, hubs of wagon wheels, and for piling at the edges of rivers and canals, and the demand for these uses did not justify high prices.

Elm's least attractive feature is its instability. It will move and twist, sometimes dramatically, with changes in humidity, and it is for this reason that it is not ideal for cabinet-making. Many makers these days will only use elm as a veneer in cabinets, gluing it on to a stable substrate such as MDF. The flexible structure of a Windsor chair, however, is ideal to cope with the instability of elm. The seat can 'move' quite significantly without compromising the integrity of the chair, and it is still a relatively common sight to find old Windsor chairs that have twisted seats, and yet function satisfactorily. The most common cause of serious warping in old chairs is the dramatic change in humidity that they were subjected to when they were first brought into a centrally heated house, and perhaps even placed adjacent to a radiator.

The fact that the elm grew outside woods managed for timber favoured its use in Windsor chairs, particularly when chairs were made by individuals. One tree could be felled and would yield twenty to forty seats, and this could keep an individual going for some time. Foresters looking after a woodland are loath to cut down a small number of trees for fear of devaluing the rest of the crop, so trees growing in hedgerows were ideal for relatively small-scale users as their removal had no impact on the value of the surrounding timber.

The early success of Windsor chairs must have been in part due to the choice of elm as the seat wood, because the grain patterns and colours are superior to any other native alternative. The dog's-tooth pattern in the grain is one of the best identifiers of the wood, even in the oldest chairs. The grain can take on wild swirling patterns, with colours from pale to dark brown, sometimes with distinct green bands. These days elm is becoming rapidly scarcer due to the ravages of Dutch elm

disease. It is very difficult to find a suitable alternative, especially one with boards wide enough for one-piece seats. The most common alternative used today is ash, which by comparison is visually second rate.

Cost and colour were not the only considerations in choosing the wood. Elm has a wild and interlocking grain, as anyone who has adzed an elm seat will know to their cost. However, this property means that splits do not propagate easily across a board. When driving legs into a seat and securing them with wedges this is a consideration – but perhaps this is a case of inventing a reason for the use of elm after the fact.

Elm varies considerably between species. For example, wych-elm (Ulmus glabra) tends to have straight grain, and the wood is denser and harder than English elm (Ulmus procera). The latter can be remarkably soft and easy to work, but the wildness of the grain will still cause challenges when worked with edge tools.

WOODS FOR OTHER PARTS

The historical choice of woods for the other parts of the chair was very broad. The finest chairs used yew, which over time develops a wonderful amber-coloured glow. Coppiced yew was used to make the arms and spindles, and larger sections were needed for cabriole legs and turnings. The arms were made by steam-bending complete stems, and then shaping them afterwards. It is possible to see many pin knots along these arms, and even more telling is the presence of the hollow pith and surrounding annual rings at the end of each hand. Pale sapwood is also sometimes visible.

A large proportion of Victorian Windsor turnings, especially those made in the Thames Valley and around High Wycombe, were made of beech, where this species can be found in abundance on the chalk Chilterns. Beech splits well, allowing the easy production of turning blanks, and its fine grain allows crisp details to be produced.

Ash was another common wood for Windsors. Ash also splits cleanly, and it has the key quality of toughness, and can be steam-bent into arms, bows, crests, crinoline stretchers and arm-posts. Ash is one of the fastest-growing trees in England, and it seeds and grows freely on chalk downland. It is not necessary for the trees to grow to maturity before they can be used, and poles of 8–9in (20–23cm) in diameter are ideal for chairmaking. A densely self-seeded stand of ash is an idea-source of chair wood. The trees will have grown rapidly and vertically as they compete to reach the light, and the complete canopy of leaves will shade the lower branches causing them to become redundant and to quickly drop off. This leads to long straight lengths of knot-free wood. Ash is another wood, like elm, that does not necessarily grow in managed woodlands, making it more accessible to early chairmakers.

The earliest Windsors often incorporated cherry and walnut for legs and arms respectively, and in other parts of the country woods such as alder and birch have been found. It is thought that cherry was a common wood in the earliest Windsors because there were many fruit orchards in the Thames valley in the early eighteenth century. This is an excellent example of the use of locally grown wood in Windsor chairs.

Cherry and walnut both have very good natural colour; they are also fine grained and are relatively soft, so can be easily shaped. The wonderful colours and patinas of these early chairs is clear proof that using these woods was a good choice. By contrast, old ash chairs tend to be rather pale and somewhat grey in colour.

America: Traditional Woods

WOODS FOR SEATS

The most common woods used in Windsor seats were pines and poplars. A few alternative woods such as chestnut and lime (basswood) were used, but they were uncommon. These woods were softer and more easily split than English elm, but much easier to work. To reduce the problems of splitting, thick boards were chosen and greater gaps were left between holes for legs and spindles, and the edges of the seat; this way, if a split began then it would not reach the edge. Both of these main seat woods were available in wide boards, largely free of knots – a perfect combination for making seats. It should be remembered that in the eighteenth century the population of America was still relatively low, and much woodland was still unexploited, unlike the old managed woodlands of England. The free availability of this wide-boarded timber is something that we can only dream of today, now that so much woodland has been felled and replanted at least once. However, the early makers did not have it all their own way, as the technology

available for harvesting and transporting the wood was primitive, and it is likely that they could only use wood grown in the locality.

The thickness of the seats and the softness of the wood may have been reasons that the American makers sculpted their seats more dramatically than their English cousins. The shield seat found in bow-backs and continuous-arm chairs is a very complex three-dimensional shape, which would not have been economic to produce unless the wood was easy to carve. It does not seem unreasonable to suggest that the choice of a relatively soft seat wood played a key role in the later success of American Windsor chairs, as comfortable, attractive and complex seat shapes could be adopted economically.

The softness of the woods, which makes for easy shaping, inevitably comes with corresponding drawbacks. The grain in pine can be most attractive, but it is not in the class of elm, and its coarseness would have detracted from the elegance of the chair designs if it had not been painted. Poplar has much less defined grain, but has a deep green colour in the heartwood, contrasting with the creamy sapwood. The tradition of painting Windsor chairs, which was imported with early English chairs, is perfect for covering the unexceptional grain of pine and poplar.

WOODS FOR OTHER PARTS

While there are exceptions, non-seat woods were used for two purposes: shaving or steam-bending (spindles, arms, crests and bows), and turning (legs, stretchers and arm-posts).

Maple was the most common turning wood, its fine grain structure allowing it to hold very crisp detail compared with the shaving/bending woods, which tended to be open-pored and coarse-grained. They tend to chip when you are trying to produce very fine detail. Maple has many similarities to English beech, and it is of no surprise that these were the major turning woods on each side of the Atlantic.

The most commonly used woods for bending and spindles were hickory, oak and ash, with a few others such as birch used occasionally. These woods grew extensively over north-east America and so were readily available for chairmaking. They could be split easily and accurately from the log and their natural toughness allowed fine spindles to be incorporated in the chairs without risk of breakage.

Toughness was a particularly important characteristic of American chairs as they had less wood in them than their equivalent English chairs. They relied on toughness and structure to produce strength, while English chairs depended more on the thickness of the wood. Ash, hickory and oak are all ideally suited to this approach.

CHOOSING NON-TRADITIONAL WOODS

As a contemporary maker you have the freedom to choose from a much wider range of woods than our forebears. If you live in an area where very few trees grow, such as the north of Scotland, then you may be unable to use any locally sourced wood. There is no need to follow the example of old chairs religiously, but it would be foolish to ignore all the lessons that are available from studying them.

Never forget that you are unlikely to find the perfect wood for any job. There are always trade-offs to be considered. Once a wood has been chosen, chairmakers tend to concentrate on

Medullary rays and annual rings are visible at right-angles to each other.

its good qualities, and live with the drawbacks provided they do not cause structural problems that will lead to unsound chairs. Sadly, poor choices may not become apparent for several years.

ALTERNATIVE WOODS

In my early years as a chairmaker I used sycamore for turnings. My local sawmill ripped left-over sycamore into 2in (5cm) squares of 2–3ft (60–90cm) in length, and sold it quite reasonably to turners such as myself. I considered that it worked and appeared similar to beech, and being readily available, it was ideal. Turning it was a real pleasure, and provided the tools were sharp, one could produce very crisp detail in legs and arm-posts. I found a way to stain it that made it attractive, and made up for the lack of grain markings. It also painted well.

My sycamore-turning phase did not last very long because the sawmill soon gave up producing the inexpensive squares and I moved on to other species. Nevertheless I felt confident that sycamore was one alternative that could be successfully used for legs.

Oak is not a traditional wood for Windsor chairmaking in England, and yet I use it for all parts other than the seat in most of the chairs that I sell. The wood has a beautiful colour and grain pattern, and it is the dominant species where I live in West Sussex. There is no need to stain chairs made from oak as it is attractive in its native state, whereas it is always difficult to achieve an attractive colour with ash, as stained ash almost always looks just that – stained.

Oak has the uncommon and distinctive feature of having pronounced medullary rays, arranged radially to the pith. When the wood is divided radially (quartered) the rays, or flecks, are exposed, giving the sought-after look of quarter-sawn oak. These rays can be a most attractive feature in a crest, but in spindles and bows they tend not to be too distinctive. However, it is in turnings that they have their best effect. Most open-grained woods will produce rings or 'bull's eyes' when they are turned, and the faces at 90 degrees will show straight lines of the pores. However, oak will produce 'bull's eyes' on four faces of a turning, as both the pores and medullary rays are cut through. Without care it is easy to confuse the radial and tangential faces of oak turnings.

WOOD SPECIES	USES	ADVANTAGES	DISADVANTAGES
Elm	Seats	Colour, grain pattern	Unstable, not now widely available
Beech	Turnings	Splits well, fine grain produces good detail	Unexciting colour and grain, in spite of medullary flecks
Yew	All parts other than seat	Colour and ease of shaping	Difficult to source. Very pale sapwood Large sections often contain flaws. Poisonous dust
Ash	All parts	Tough, easy to cleave, steam-bends very well. Shaves well when partially dried	Colour, stringy grain makes shaving difficult across wavy grain. Wood from large trees less tough than from smaller trees
Cherry	Turnings, splats, seats	Colour improves and darkens with age. Turns very well	Boards not very wide, chips easily (somewhat brittle on edges). Expensive
Black walnut	Seats	Colour	Soft. Not wide boards Expensive
English walnut	Bows	Bends well	Difficult to source
Sycamore	Turnings	Fine grain and hardness gives very crisp turnings	Unexciting grain and colour
Sweet chestnut	Turnings, Spindles, Bows	Splits very easily. Coppiced wood readily available in some areas. Can be steam-bent. Shaves well. Can be fumed with ammonia	Soft. Difficult to find lengths over 3ft (90cm) long free of knots, and straight
Oak	All parts other than seat	Colour and grain. Splits easily. Shaves very well. Steam-bends in less time than ash. Readily available in many areas	Expensive. Shrinks greatly and asymmetrically on drying, with a tendency to split
Pine	Seats	Quality pine produces fine seats. Easy to work	Relatively low strength. Coarse grain pattern
Poplar/Tulip	Seats	Easy to work. Inexpensive. Paints very well	Relatively low strength and soft. Does not stain well. Colour of heart wood green (eventually turns brown)
Hickory	Spindles and bows	Tough like ash. Bends well	
Maple	Turnings	Hard wood and fine grain gives excellent detail	Uninteresting grain and colour. Good for painted chairs

These patterns and the natural colour are enough to make oak a good choice for chairmaking, but it also steam-bends well and is easy to shape into spindles. However, it is not perfect. If green (wet) oak is turned into legs, then it is very prone to splitting as it dries, though wet sanding, described in the next chapter, reduces this tendency. It also shrinks far more tangentially than radially. Every wood has its drawbacks, but you must learn to live with them and work around them.

Beech and cherry also have visible medullary rays, but they are much finer than those in oak, and can be seen as very fine flecks rather than the much coarser markings of oak.

This is not to decry using ash and other woods without significant medullary rays; it is just that you should be aware of, and make the most of, all the features of any wood that you use.

Another wood that can be used is sweet chestnut (*Castanea sativa*). This is found on sandy soils close to where I live, in the form of chestnut coppice. The wood used to be used for fencing, but this trade has almost died out, and apart from small quantities used for walking sticks, much has recently been cut for pulp. There are, however, many enterprising people developing new uses and markets for the wood, and one of the most promising appears to be to produce high quality woodchip for carbon-neutral heating. I find it an excellent wood for turning, and it has the useful quality of minimal shrinkage. It can also be readily steam-bent, provided a sufficient length without knots can be found. Its drawbacks are that it splits very readily (this can be an advantage), and it is relatively soft.

The lesson to be learned from my use of non-traditional woods for Windsors is that it is worth experimenting with different and particularly locally grown timber. Most woods will be suitable for at least part of a Windsor chair, and it makes for a much easier life if your wood is readily available. The wood will not have travelled as far, your chairmaking will be a more environmentally sustainable activity, and the wood is likely to be less expensive. Even more importantly, local customers will appreciate furniture made from local materials.

Wet or Dry Wood?

The majority of woodworkers have probably never seriously considered this question. Dry wood is all that is available from the sawmill or timber store, so that is what is used; and in practice most modern woodworking depends on the avail-

ability of dry wood. Dry wood can be machined and it will maintain its dimensions within a narrow range; it can be stored indefinitely, and most woods are readily available from a range of outlets.

Why would you want to use wet wood that shrinks and splits and still has the bark attached, which probably harbours a thriving flora and fauna? One answer is that this is how the original makers of Windsor chairs used their wood, and so that is how we should do it, too. Indeed, if your intention is to replicate old chairs in every detail then you will need to replicate the work methods as well, and you may gain great satisfaction from researching old tools and work methods. Furthermore, if you are a purist you will shun electricity for power tools, and if you wish to be absolutely genuine you will forego any artificial heat or light!

This approach is somewhat extreme, and involves a whole change in lifestyle in order to recreate and experience the life and work of an early chairmaker. History enthusiasts may wish to pursue it, and the lessons learned may be profound, provided that enough time is available to become a sufficiently knowledgeable chairmaker to be able to interpret the clues that have been left behind. However, if you are a modern woodworker with a workshop full of the latest high quality power tools you may take the position that you are going to create Windsor chairs using your existing tools, and you will use dry wood because that is what they are designed to work with. This is a perfectly valid approach, but it is unlikely that you will be able to create chairs with the same vitality as the originals.

Working with Green Wood

Working with wet, or green, wood has many advantages, which I will detail below, but the most important is that it is the route to producing the finest Windsors possible. It is not a lifestyle choice, though it can be made into one, but a rational decision made in pursuit of the finest chairs.

Green woodworking has been promoted by many people over the last forty years, and it is probably the pole-lathe enthusiasts in England that have done more than any to achieve the awareness that it has today. Their re-creation of the life of the bodgers, who worked in the woods around High Wycombe turning legs and stretchers, has inspired many to adopt green woodworking. However, the pole-lather's success means that green woodworking is inextricably associated in most people's minds with working out of doors with no electricity. This approach may suit many people, but it is perfectly sensible to work green wood in a well lit, heated workshop containing plenty of power tools, while listening to music on the radio! This is how I choose to work.

So how do you work with green wood, and why? Working with green wood is a three-step process: first the piece is shaped, leaving the tenons oversize; then it is dried; and finally the tenons are accurately sized. It may take a couple of days to make and dry a leg using green wood, but the tree from which the leg is turned could have been felled on that same day, and so the timespan between standing tree and finished chair can be as little as three days. Alternatively if you buy and use dry wood, then the time between felling and use is hidden, but is reflected in the cost.

The advantages of using green wood fall into four main categories:

• Sourcing and cost
• Minimal dust
• Use of splitting rather than sawing
• Ease of shaping

Undercutting the oak.

After removing approximately 12in (30cm) of buttress, the tree yielded two 7ft 6in (2.3m) lengths of chairmaking wood. Not a perfect specimen, but acceptable. Total volume 25cu ft (0.7m³). Two 8ft (2.4m) sections were also taken from the same tree for gate posts.

SOURCING AND COST

Since the wood is bought directly from the woodland, with no intervening processes, it is much less expensive than sawn dry timber. The benefit to the woodland owner is the ability to turn his trees directly into cash rather than having to deal with a timber merchant or saw mill and haggle over the cost for the whole wood. The down side for the owner is that you are looking for only the best trees. However, if you can use species that do not have a significant value (such as ash in England), you will hopefully come to an arrangement that is beneficial to both sides.

If you can find exactly what you are looking for, it is worth paying a good price, and one that will dispose the owner to having you come back time and again. By all means shop around, but a good relationship with someone who takes an interest in, and understands what you do, is worth a lot. For example, unless they really understand what you mean by 'straight', and why it is so important, you will always be offered second-rate timber.

The ideal situation is to be able to go into a wood and choose the tree to be felled. You will be looking for the perfect tree, but do not be disappointed if you cannot find it and have to compromise slightly. Unfortunately only experience will tell you how much you can compromise without choosing wood that proves to be useless for chairmaking. In any event, choose the very best that you can find.

So what makes a 'perfect' tree for green woodworking? First the tree should be growing vertically. If it is growing at an angle, then the wood on one side of the tree will be in com-

pression and the other side in tension. When the wood dries it is likely to bend, which is a problem if you are making legs!

Second, you should avoid a tree that has grown in a spiral; some trees can have up to 45 degrees of twist over 8–10ft (2.5–3m). The only clue that this has happened is in the bark: if it shows a twist then reject the tree, even if everything else is perfect. Twisted wood is fine for short pieces such as legs and spindles, but it makes life very difficult when making bows, which may be 60in (1.5m) or more in length.

Finally – and most obviously – there should not be any knots visible on the surface of the length that you are buying. A knot, or former branch, distorts the wood around it, sometimes for a considerable distance. The effect on ash can persist for many years of growth, while oak straightens up much more quickly. The knots do not have to be large to cause problems. Oak often has epicormic growth, which translates into pin-knots in the wood. These are not just on the surface, but may travel back into the wood for a significant distance. The presence of these small knots can add to the character of the wood for cabinet makers, but should be avoided at all costs by the green woodworker.

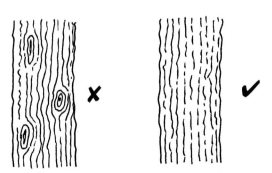

Knots will cause bent grain and make shaping split wood impossible.

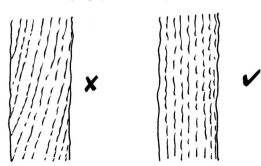

Avoid trees where the bark shows a spiral pattern up the tree.

The tree must not be leaning, otherwise some wood will be in tension and other in compression.

A knot, however small, weakens the piece that you are making; if the piece is very fine (for example, a spindle) or is to be subjected to great stress (for example, steam-bending a bow), then it can lead to failure. Avoid knots altogether if you can.

If you cannot find a woodland owner who will let you choose your own tree, then you could seek out a tree surgeon. Do not choose someone who only works in suburban gardens, as he will never find the timber you are looking for; instead seek out someone who works in the countryside, and preferably cuts firewood in the winter. They will have access to woodland, and if you can interest them in your work they will look out for the type of wood you need.

Finally, as a last resort, you can go to a sawmill and ask to look through their woodpile. Inevitably this will be the most expensive option, as considerable effort will have been expended to get it to the mill, and they will want to get their money back and make a profit.

In fact, the price of wood is not as important as you may think. Quality is the first consideration. If you have chosen well then wastage will be minimal, but as the quality deteriorates so the wastage increases, and the wood soon becomes a liability rather than an asset.

MINIMAL DUST

While working with green wood there is no dust created at all that can enter your lungs and cause respiratory problems. Shaving produces clean cuts, and even if you do take a saw to the wood, the sawdust will never become airborne because it is so damp and heavy. A bandsaw is useful for producing bending blanks from green wood, but no dust extraction is necessary. Turning green wood also produces no dust, just large quantities of wet chips.

BANDSAWING GREEN WOOD

This is a very useful technique, but not without challenges of its own. Nevertheless these can all be overcome, and should not stop you from using this method. Green wood can be cut on a bandsaw with a coarse blade. However, unless the piece is square there is a risk that as the blade moves through the wood the surface in contact with the table will change, causing the wood to rotate and jam the blade, or at least slow it.

With sustained use, wet sawdust will collect on the inside of the blade, being compressed each time it passes over the bandsaw's wheels. If this is allowed to accumulate too much, the blade will begin to move on the wheel and will eventually fall off, ruining itself on the metal guards of the tool. Cutting out a couple of seats in dry wood will remove the build-up, and prevent problems.

Finally, the wet sawdust from the wood will tend to clog up the guides and generally increase the amount of friction. Briefly running a bar of beeswax along the back edge of the blade can free it. Note that a smaller bandsaw will be more susceptible to all of these problems than a larger machine.

The surface left after turning, sawing or shaving will need to be cleaned up at some point before the piece is incorporated into the chair, but this can be achieved with the minimum of dust (these techniques are described in the next chapter). Spindles do not need to be sanded at all if they are finished carefully with a spokeshave; steam-bent pieces can be scraped and shaved with minimal sanding; and turnings can be sanded while still wet (no dust), requiring only the briefest of sanding

¾in (12mm) blade, three teeth per inch, skip-tooth pattern, suitable for sawing green wood.

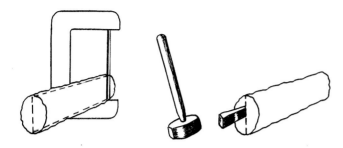

Wood can be converted with either a bandsaw or by splitting.

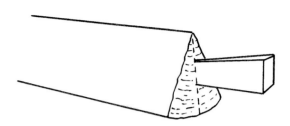

When splitting wood halve it with the wedge to have best chance of the split running true.

when dry.

Everything should be done to avoid making dust in the workshop in the first place. Green woodworking can play a very significant role in minimizing dust production and therefore reducing the chances of developing health problems associated with dust.

SPLITTING VERSUS SAWING

Dry wood is almost always roughly dimensioned using a saw, but in green woodworking the saw is used mainly to cut the wood to the correct length. Reduction of the other dimensions is made by splitting the wood. This process starts with the complete tree trunk, and progresses until a piece has been produced that can be shaped by finer tools such as the drawknife, spokeshave or lathe. Some woods, such as oak, can be split accurately down to small dimensions, but with others such as ash, where the split may have a greater tendency to wander, it may be better to saw the roughly split wood along the grain to produce the finer pieces.

Splitting wood along the grain is the key process in green woodworking. If the grain runs the length of the piece, then it will have the maximum strength possible. It also means that it can be made finer than if made with wood where the grain runs out along its length. Not all chairs need to be fine and light in weight and looks, but it is never beneficial for a chair to contain much unnecessary weight. 'Less is more' is a good principle to bear in mind when making Windsor chairs, and making them with green wood allows one to achieve this ideal more easily.

Larger pieces, such as the original tree, can be split using a 7lb (3kg) short-handled sledgehammer and wedges, or with a froe, which is initially hit with a club and then twisted to propagate

the split. Use of these tools will be discussed in the next chapter.

EASE OF SHAPING: DRY AND WET WOOD

It is well known that dry oak is hard, and this hardness only increases with age. What is not so well known is what it is like when it is fresh and wet. It is a revelation to take a drawknife to green oak for the first time when making a spindle: the texture of the wood is more akin to a vegetable, such as a carrot, and the wood seems to crackle as the blade is drawn through it.

Not all woods feel the same, but they are all much softer and easier to shape when wet. Shaping that might take minutes to achieve with a plane on dried wood can be done in seconds with a drawknife on wet wood; and if you are seeking a really flat surface, then a plane can still be used on the wet wood, though by the time it has dried it will probably no longer be flat!

The speed and ease with which wood can be shaped when wet is a compelling argument in favour of green woodworking. Even more important is the fact that the end product will look as though it has been created by hand, which is a feature that has considerable economic value in a machine-based world.

Another benefit of working soft wood is that tools stay sharper for longer. If time is not an issue in your chairmaking then resharpening is a minor inconvenience, but if you make to sell, then this saving in time will save you money. In earlier times the quality of steel available to artisans was not as good as it is today, and the use of soft wood was probably the only way in which wood could be shaped without having constantly to resharpen the tools.

This book will describe the making of all parts of the chair from green wood, other than the seat. However there is some evidence that the elm seats of old English chairs were adzed while they were still wet and soft, and then left to dry before use. This makes sense, particularly if you have ever attempted to adze an elm seat: it is hard work! If the wood were shaped before it had dried and developed a moisture gradient across its thickness, then it would remain fairly flat. If, however, it had already partially dried, then hollowing out the top surface would have exposed wetter wood, which would have shrunk more than the underneath of the seat, causing the seat to curl towards the top surface.

DRYING GREEN WOOD

Pieces that have been shaped while wet need to be dried before being incorporated into the chair. This process can be as simple or as elaborate as you wish. An airing cupboard (around the household hot-water cylinder – if present) makes an excellent drying space, but may not be universally popular. If time is no object, then keeping the pieces in a dry, and preferably warm, room will achieve the same effect, but will take longer.

If you have a lot of wood to dry, then a cabinet containing a heater (for example, an oil-filled radiator) is ideal. Make sure that there is access for cold dry air to enter the cabinet, and an exit hole for the hot wet air to escape. A fan will circulate the air in the cabinet and prevent the hot air collecting at the top, and the bottom of the cabinet remaining cool. Insulation of the cabinet and a thermostat will both reduce energy usage. If this specification is still not sufficient, then a dehumidifier could also be incorporated inside the cabinet, though I have found this to be unnecessary. Finally, it is worth having a thermometer, such as a meat thermometer, inserted through the side of the cabinet to keep track of the temperature inside.

Unfortunately not all woods can be dried at the same rate without causing damage such as splitting. For example, ash and sweet chestnut can be dried very aggressively with no problems – eg. by using an insulated cabinet kept at up to 50°C and a dehumidifier. Oak, however, will not react well to

Drying cabinet, insulated to retain heat. An oil-filled radiator provides the heat, and a fan circulates the air to prevent stratification.

ACIDIC WOOD

Some woods such as oak contain acids that affect steel. A tool that has been shaping oak for a while takes on a bluey-black colour, and this can be transferred to your fingers as well. In fact it can take two days for the colour to come off one's fingertips after a day's turning of oak! Some people worry that their tools will become pitted by the tannic acid in oak, but in my experience if they are kept in a dry environment there is no need to clean them off after use.

these conditions.

Oak legs need to be dried over a period of approximately three weeks to minimize splitting: one week outdoors, shaded from the sun and sheltered from excessively drying winds; one week in a cool dry room; and finally one week in a warm dry room. Splits form because the outside of the piece is drying and shrinking faster than the inside, but over time they will disappear altogether once the whole thickness is dry.

Trial and error is probably your best guide for developing your own system for drying wood, but weighing the components regularly will give a guide as to how drying is progressing.

STORING WOOD

If the key feature of green woodworking is that the wood is wet, then the key aim of storage is to maintain the moisture in the wood until it is needed. The biggest enemies of stored green wood are the sun, followed by wind.

Ideally you would store your wood close to where it will be used, and also in a place easily accessible by vehicle (assuming that you bring the wood home on a trailer). Wet wood is heavy, and great care must be taken in handling it to avoid injury to yourself and others. The size of individual log that you select will be determined both by how many chairs you intend to make and how large a tree you can physically handle. With ingenuity it is remarkable how large a log can be moved with aids such as winches, but there is always a risk of injury if a log rolls out of control.

Storing wood against a north-facing wall is a good way of minimizing the amount of direct sunlight. If this is not possible, you will have to create shade in another way. Just covering wood with a tarpaulin is not sufficient: this will keep off a drying wind, but will not prevent significant heating from the sun, which can create an atmosphere (warm and wet) under the sheet, perfect for the growth of wood-rotting fungi.

When you first get your wood home, paint the cut ends to minimize moisture loss through the ends. This is where your log will lose the greatest amount of water if you do not take this basic precaution, and splits will soon develop all over unpainted end grain. These splits will then begin to move into the log, with the risk that if the log has been cut close to the maximum length that is required (for example, 60in/1.5m for a bow-back chair bow), it will no longer be possible to make this key piece once the dry split ends have been removed.

Do not cover the log with a sheet until after it has been split. Provided the ends have been painted and it has been kept in the shade, it will keep in good condition for many months. Just think of saw mills that buy their logs in the autumn and may not finish sawing them until the following summer, but keep their wood exposed to the elements in the meantime. However, once split, the log will lose water very quickly form the exposed surfaces, and a sheet to prevent evaporation may become essential.

Oak should kept as wet as possible before use as it becomes much more difficult to shape when it dries and hardens. Ash by contrast works better when it has lost some of its natural moisture. I prefer to split ash logs a week or so before I want to use them, leaving them exposed to the air to lower their water content.

If at all possible keep stored wood away from contact with soil. Soil contains fungi and bacteria that would just love to get into your wood, so don't give them the chance: if you have to store it over soil, put it on bearers so it is lifted off the ground by a few inches. This also helps to keep the bark clean, which can be important if the log needs to be cut with a chainsaw.

Finally, do not forget that a freshly felled log is still alive. I have occasionally put such logs under a tarpaulin and come back a few days later to find that they have sprouted fresh shoots along their length!

Ends of oak logs were painted with household emulsion paint within one hour of felling to reduce moisture loss from the cut ends.

WASTE

There is always waste produced from woodworking, and green woodworking is no different; however, it is wet, and comes in all shapes and sizes. These days when we are more aware of the need to consider the effect of our activities on the environment, dealing with waste is a serious consideration.

When the tree is cut down, it is to be hoped that the crown of the tree will be used, as well as the clear trunk that is going to be made into chairs. If the tree is tall, then beams may be made from the trunk beyond the first branch, and the remainder is most likely to be used as firewood. If your woodland source is a member of the Forest Stewardship Council (FSC) scheme, then you can be sure that new trees will be planted in place of the one cut down. However, unless you are the woodland owner yourself, the remainder of the tree is not your responsibility.

The amount of waste will be affected most by the quality and the species of wood that you have bought. Oak has a significant band of pale sapwood under the bark which is useless for chairmaking and will have to be discarded. It is far weaker than heartwood, and is highly susceptible to attack by fungi and insects. Ash, by contrast, has no obvious sapwood, and the wood can be used right up to the bark.

The proportion of sapwood in an oak log decreases as the girth increases, so it may be better value to purchase a larger rather than a smaller log. However, woodland owners are unlikely to wish to fell immature oak trees, so there may be little choice in the matter! If you buy square-edged sawn timber you will not be so aware of waste because most of it will have been dealt with by the sawmill – but green woodworkers have it all to deal with.

Waste will come in several forms, some of which are easier to dispose of that others:

Solid wood: Off-cuts from the log where the ends have dried out and are of no use; lengths of wood affected by knots; and wood that has split too thin for use. All these can be cut to manageable lengths, if necessary, and burned for heating once dry.

Sapwood and bark: Irregular shaped pieces split off with a froe. Either dry and burn these, or compost them over time.

Shavings: Waste from the drawknife and spokeshaves. This dries very quickly as it is thin, but it takes up a large volume because each piece tends to curl up. This is not so easy to store and burn, but it is possible.

Chippings: Waste from turning. These are wet because of the nature of the wood, and are hard to dry because they pack together so tightly. Their use for animal bedding is precluded due to the moisture (though there is no dust to worry about) and small quantities could be used for smoking food, but this would never deal with more than an occasional chair's worth of waste. Probably the best use is to compost the chippings, and eventually to incorporate the compost into the soil. The wood will need nitrogen for it to be broken down, and incorporation of animal manure will help the process. Some users put the chippings directly on to flowerbeds as a mulch to reduce moisture loss and reduce weed growth, but this will tend to draw nitrogen away from the soil and growing plants.

In conclusion, you need to think about how to deal with the waste before embarking seriously on green woodworking, otherwise you will soon be overwhelmed.

The Workshop

The first essential in a workshop is good lighting, and guarded fluorescent strips are ideal as their length helps to reduce shadows. It is difficult to have too much light, and you will really appreciate it when working at more detailed operations. Natural daylight is beneficial, but try to avoid direct sunlight as it casts very dark shadows and will heat and dry any wood on which it falls, leading to possible splitting and bending. Blinds on all but north-facing windows are a big advantage. Finally, if fluorescent lighting is chosen, be sure to select 'daylight' tubes as these will produce a much more pleasant working environment, with the advantage that colours will be the same indoors and out.

Turning under fluorescent tubes alone can be risky because the strobe effect of the light can make a turning piece appear stationary at certain revolutions. An additional incandescent light source will help to eliminate this problem.

The amount of space needed is hard to determine. To misquote C. Northcote Parkinson, 'Work expands to fit the space available'. A small garage should be quite adequate, and if you are a very tidy person you could probably cope with much less. The largest item in your workshop is likely to be your bench, and it should be possible to make a chair on a bench no more than 24in (60cm) square. Whatever the size of the bench, it will be most useful if it can be placed in the centre of the workshop rather than against a wall.

If you plan to work throughout the year, then insulation of your workshop may be essential to prevent it becoming either too hot or cold. The workshop should also be dry. Insulation and dryness will produce a pleasant working environment with minimum energy usage, and no risk of condensation.

If the environment is not comfortable there may be unexpected consequences. It is quite possible to work in a cold workshop if plenty of clothes are worn, but you may find, for example, that glues do not work unless they and the wood are at more than 10°C.

If you plan to spend many hours in your workshop then a good floor is essential. In any event make it flat to avoid trip-

Types of wood waste

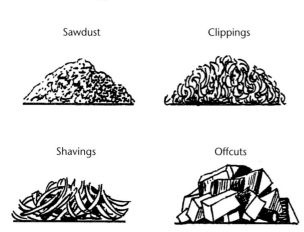

Sawdust

Clippings

Shavings

Offcuts

Waste will have to be considered – offcuts, shavings and chippings.

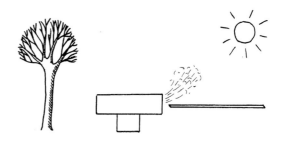

Steambending is best done outdoors to keep the moisture out of the workshop.

ping, but a wooden surface will be warmer and more comfortable than concrete in the longer term.

It is unlikely that all chairmaking tasks will be carried out in the workshop. Some processes, such as splitting wood, require space to swing a sledgehammer. Others, such as steam-bending, generate large quantities of water vapour, which could play havoc with a dry workshop.

If the weather is fine, then there is no reason why these jobs should not be carried on outside, but if space is available then a shelter from the elements will allow chairmaking to continue every day of the year.

Tools and Equipment

BENCH

The bench is at the heart of any workshop. It needs to be solid, at the correct height, and be designed in such a way that chair parts can be easily secured. A flat top (no tool tray) is a great advantage so that one can work in any position, and particularly at the corners.

This small bench has a (detachable) shave-horse mechanism mounted on it. Spindles can be shaved while standing, and they can be held both horizontally and vertically by the same mechanism.

DESIGNING A BENCH

There are endless designs available that can be made or bought, but if you are starting from scratch I would urge you to build your own using the following design. It is simple, quick and inexpensive to make, but it has proved ideal for chairmaking over many years.

The key features are a box construction that gives enormous rigidity, and a plywood top with a generous overhang all round. It can be put together in a few hours using plywood, planed softwood, and a generous number of woodscrews (all readily available from a builder's merchant). Fitting a vice can take as long as making the bench itself.

The top should be 25mm WBP plywood. One layer is adequate, two is luxury. If a 4 x 4ft bench (or smaller) is planned and a full sheet (8 x 4ft) has to be bought, then the second layer can be made from the single sheet. It will add considerably to the mass of the bench, and can be considered a sacrificial layer, although I am nowhere near replacing mine after twelve years of intense use.

Legs can be made from 4 x 4in p.a.r. (planed all round) softwood, and intermediate supports from 2 x 2in p.a.r. softwood. The panels are ideally cut from 18mm softwood sheathing ply (otherwise known as spruce plywood). This is relatively inexpensive, has one good face, and is easy to cut with a hand saw.

Make up two end panels using 50 x 5mm screws, and join these together with two more sheets of 18mm ply. Screw 2 x 2in all the way round the top of the bench (between each leg) to provide an apron on to which the top can be screwed.

Countersink and screw the top to the apron, leaving a minimum 2in (5cm) overhang at each leg; and fit a vice close to a leg on a long side.

Although the resulting bench will be quite heavy, it may be worth attaching the legs to the floor with small brackets to prevent it moving it during vigorous shaving.

VICE

As with benches, so there is a very wide range of vices available. The most flexible vice, and one that is ideally suited to holding irregularly shaped pieces, is the pattern maker's vice. The jaws can move in and out of parallel, swivel in the vertical plane, and the whole body can be rotated from the vertical to horizontal. It is possible to use a standard woodworking vice, but the extra flexibility of the pattern maker's vice is valuable and should be carefully considered if buying a vice for the first time.

Many chairmakers hold most of their wood using a shave horse. Personally I prefer to stand, and can work more effectively in this way. A bench is always useful, whatever you are making, while a shave horse has limited uses.

When shaping the seat, it needs to be held horizontally and securely on the bench. The overhang on my bench design allows for it to be clamped to the top, and often across a corner of the bench. Speed clamps (that use the same principle as mastic guns) are inexpensive, strong, and can be used one-handed, and are ideal for this purpose where re-clamping is frequently needed. However, sometimes the clamps get in the way of working, and then a system of dogs is ideal. Locate these diagonally from a corner and drill new holes as required in the top. You should have no qualms about drilling new holes in a plywood top, whereas it would require great conviction to do the same in a fine cabinet maker's bench top.

Tools and Equipment

If you are already a woodworker it is likely that you will need to add a small number of hand tools, but will be able to avoid major investment. However, if Windsor chairmaking is your

Simply made bench ideally suited to chairmaking. Note the pattern-maker's vice mounted on the plywood top.

first venture into woodworking then you will need to give careful thought as to how you set up your workshop.

Hand Tools or Power Tools?

Electricity versus manual labour: is this laziness, or a great idea? This book is dedicated to making Windsor furniture by hand, so why contemplate using anything other than hand tools? This question is almost the same in practice as 'why use electricity?', and the answer depends on whether your aim is to make the best possible furniture, or to adopt a particular method of making that coincides with your views on environment and lifestyle choices. My preference is for the former, and I will use whatever tools I can find that will help me to make the finest chairs.

The question of whether to use power tools is an old chestnut, and any discussion usually ends up with the statement that 'makers in the eighteenth century would have used them if they had been available', because they were making the chairs to make money. It is possibly to our great benefit that power tools were not available then, as their products might well have been poorer for it. It is one thing to mechanize a process that has previously only been done by hand, and quite another to consider what a product might have looked like (if it had ever developed) if machinery and electricity had been available in the 1700s.

Windsor chairs were the product of hand tools, and much of their appeal derives from this fact: their lack of engineering 'perfection' makes them pleasing to the human eye. Therefore to capture the essence of the old chairs, even in new designs, you should be careful in choosing the techniques that are used. In my opinion you should avoid the use of jigs that allow the making of identical pieces repeatedly. The only jig that I use that breaks this rule is a tilting table on the pillar drill to drill repeatable holes for the legs, arm-posts and bows in the seat (*see* page 40). Every other process is guided by hand and eye, and this applies to using the bandsaw, lathe and the use of cordless drills to make some of the holes.

Another example of this philosophy in practice can be seen in the hollowing of seats. The adze is the traditional tool of choice for removing the bulk of the wood, but it is hard physical work and quite slow on hardwoods. If more than one seat is to be made, a blade such as the Arbortech fitted to an angle grinder speeds the process enormously. I can completely rough out an elm seat in twelve minutes when it might take twenty minutes of hard labour with an adze just to hollow the top. The Arbortech is guided by hand and eye in the same way as the adze – it is just much quicker. The down side of such a tool is that it is possible to make bigger mistakes more quickly!

It is likely that your choice of tool will change over time as you gain more experience, but provided any change does not compromise the final chair, and speeds up the process or enhances it, then change is good.

Bandsaw

As I have already suggested, a bandsaw is invaluable to the chairmaker. Of course you can do without one, but if it is in your workshop it will be used all the time and will save hours of work. It should be capable of cutting out 2in (5cm) thick hardwood seat blanks easily. Otherwise the best advice is, 'The bigger the better'. A coarse blade is essential if you plan to cut green wood, to prevent the blade clogging in the kerf. A bandsaw can be used for the following:

- Cutting out seats
- Ripping bow blanks to size
- Trimming legs to length
- Cutting green wood blanks to length
- Trimming leg tenons
- Making wedges
- Evening up leg blanks
- Cutting kerfs in leg tenons
- Shaping a crest

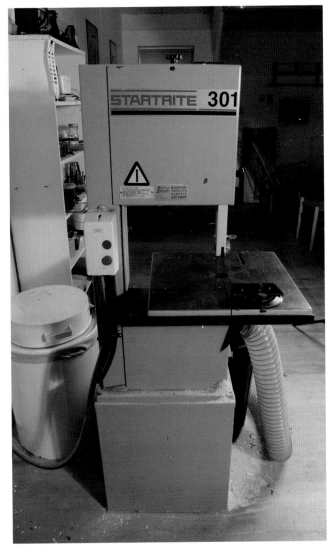

Saw with 6in (15cm) depth of cut. This has worked reliably for the past fifteen years. A larger and more powerful machine would be ideal.

Pillar Drill

As with the bandsaw, chairs can be made without a pillar drill, but having one will save considerable time and lead to more accurately made chairs. It can be used to drill the main holes in the seat, and can also be used to clean up surfaces of bows and crests when fitted with a drum sander. The table at right angles to the drill is its key feature. Before buying one, check that there is at least 6in (15cm) between pillar and drill, and make sure that there is no play in the main bearings – hold a drill bit fitted into the chuck, and if you can move it from side to side at all, reject the machine. Again, 'the bigger the better' is a good principle when choosing a machine.

A heavy-duty pillar drill with simple tilting table clamped to its table. The angle is adjusted by moving wooden blocks in and out – simple but effective.

A tilting table should be made up from two sheets of stiff and stable material, such as MDF joined together with two hinges. The tilting table should be clamped to the drill's horizontal table, and adjusted to the correct angle with blocks. Abrasive glued to one face of the blocks will prevent them from slipping during drilling. Set the angle using a protractor sitting on the tilting surface, and registering it against the straight shank of your drill. There are many more sophisticated means of setting the angle, such as wedges of set angles, but you will find that blocks work satisfactorily.

The tilting table must have a centre line that is aligned with the tip of the drill, and it will be essential to extend this centre line beyond the front edge of the table – note the aluminium angle extension in the photograph.

Lathe

Chair legs can be turned on a small and unsophisticated lathe. Legs will be no more than 2in (5cm) finished diameter, and back posts may reach to 30in (75cm) in extreme cases. The minimum requirements are:

- 2–3in (5–7.5cm) over the bed
- The ability to turn up to 24–30in (60–75cm) in length
- 450w motor
- Three speeds

A larger lathe will be heavier, and will dampen out vibrations from imperfectly balanced workpieces. It will have a more powerful motor (ideally 750w or more) that cannot be slowed down however aggressively you turn. Continuously variable speed is far from essential, as 1500–2000rpm is ideal for most chair turning, while a slow speed of around 400rpm suits a

A lathe is no use without turning tools, and the following tools will be needed:

Essential	Optional
¾in roughing gouge	Spindle gouge (larger)
Diamond-shaped parting tool	Spindle gouge (smaller)
Skew chisel	Bowl gouge – small

trapping plane. If there is any chance that you may want to use the lathe for turning more than chair parts then select the biggest and heaviest lathe possible.

Other Large Machinery

Most Windsor chair seats require a board with a width of 17in (43cm) or more. Finding boards of this width (usually in 2in/5cm thickness) is not easy, and it may be necessary to join two or more boards together to achieve the width. Unless you plan to do this entirely by hand, some large machinery will be necessary to joint and thickness the boards/seat. If you do not have this machinery yourself it may be best to find a local cabinetmaker to joint up and thickness seat blanks for you, so that you can concentrate on making the chairs.

The joints are not reinforced with biscuits or dowels because these would be exposed when the seat is hollowed. As a result the strength of the joint depends on the two surfaces being an almost perfect match, and the glue itself. Saw millers may make up wide boards for customers for table or bar tops, but these are unlikely ever to be subjected to the stresses and strains of a chair seat. Check the quality of the joints that they achieve very carefully before asking them to make up your

Jointing tulip boards to make up a seat. Care is taken to match grain and colour where possible.

Tea urn

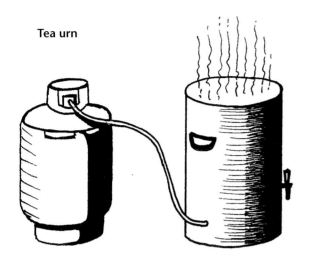

One way of generating steam for a long period (4 – 5 hours) is to use a tea urn with a water capacity of 20 litres. These can be powered by gas or electricity. Gas makes the equipment independent of an electrical supply.

A gas-fired tea urn develops the steam for the insulated box that sits directly on top. Note the arm blank ready for steaming, and the digital alarm for setting the time.

seats. They may also try to persuade you to accept a finger-type joint to maximize the surface area. Avoid this at all costs as it will lead to unsightly transitions between boards when the seat is shaped. A high-quality cabinet maker is your best bet for this demanding task if you are not in a position to do it yourself.

An 18in (45cm) planer and 20in (50cm) thicknesser are ideal for this job, as the individual boards and the glued-up blanks can be thicknessed by machine. A 12in (30cm) planer/thicknesser would do the job provided you are prepared to plane the glued-up board by hand.

Steam Generator

Steam is required for steam-bending and there are many ways of producing it. It is essential to have enough steam so that the piece to be bent is held as close to 100°C as possible. If the heat loss from the steaming process is too great and/or there is insufficient steam, then bending will not be successful.

For very small pieces a kettle might generate enough steam, but the volume of water is not great and there would be a risk of it boiling dry and damaging the kettle. Nor is refilling it with water during a steam-bending session ideal, as the water will take time to return to the boil and the piece will fall in temperature for a while, making timing difficult. The water could be topped up with boiling water, but this could be easier said than done. A larger reservoir is ideal.

The other piece of household equipment that is often considered for generating steam is a wallpaper stripper. These produce copious amounts of steam, but for a limited time; even heavy-duty strippers run out after about an hour. If you plan to steam one piece for less than an hour then this could be ideal, but it is good policy to make a series of bends at one time so that failures can be replaced and spares held in stock for future chairs. The set-up time for steam-bending may be considerable, particularly if the equipment is not permanently available, and it makes sense to spread this time over as many pieces as possible.

A tea urn holding approximately 4.5gal (20ltr) of water is an ideal solution to this problem. It may be powered by gas or electricity, and once it is boiling (note that it may take up to one hour to start boiling) it will generate steam for four hours or more. The heat source usually rated at approximately 3kW is ideal for this purpose. A steam box can be designed to sit on top of the boiler with direct access for the steam through a hole in its base.

MAKING A STEAM BOX

These days when many more people are taking up green woodworking it is possible to purchase a ready-made steam box. However, a box can be very simple to make and will cost little money. Plastic and steel tubes are popular as they have no seams along their length, and steam can be inserted at one end. If using a pipe, consider insulation – this is vital if it is a metal pipe, both for safety and to achieve the necessary temperature. Support plastic pipes along their length as they will tend to sag as they heat up. A minimum diameter of 6in will work, but 8in is preferable.

A simple but very effective box can be made from one sheet of 18mm sheathing ply. Cut four 10 x 66in (25 x 168cm) strips and screw them together to make a box. Plane the edges first to ensure a snug fit along their length; silicone bathroom sealer will improve the joint further. Then block off one end, and produce a removable lid for the other end (not too tight fitting, as it will expand with the steam). Make a suitable hole for the steam to enter, depending on the generator used.

This design will work well for a large number of bends, particularly if it is allowed to dry at the end of each session. However, over time the plywood will become more porous, and increasing amounts of heat will be lost from the box, leading to a fall in temperature inside. A longer-lasting and more sophisticated version of this box would have a second skin of plywood to act as extra insulation, and this could be improved yet further by sandwiching a vapour barrier (polythene) between the two layers, or even a layer of building insulation.

The lengths to which you go to make a steam box will depend on how frequently you expect to use it. Perhaps the best advice is to start simple, and to make improvements as necessary and as your experience and knowledge increases.

Brake

A brake, sometimes referred to as a 'riving brake', is an arrangement that allows you to hold a long piece of wood at a comfortable height so that it can be sawn or split. It is particularly valuable when you need to steer a split along a piece of wood.

As with everything else in chairmaking, there are countless ways of constructing a brake. The simplest arrangement for a

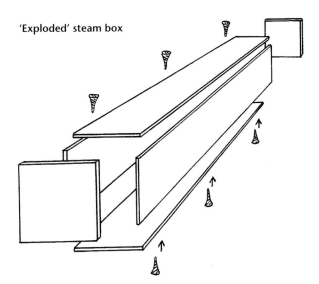

'Exploded' steam box

A steam box can be simply made by screwing together plywood from just one 8' x 4' sheet. Insulation can improve performance.

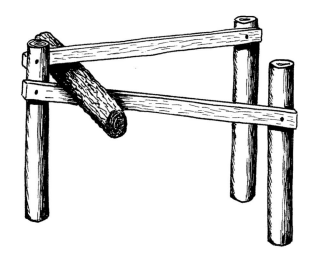

Every green woodworker should have a brake to hold wood off the gound for splitting. It allows pressure to be put on the wood during splitting to steer the split back towards the centre line if it begins to wander.

fixed brake involves driving three posts securely into the ground and then attaching two poles between them. One post has both poles attached to it, while their ends are attached to the two other vertical posts. The front pole is horizontal to the ground at a convenient height, while the back pole diverges from the front pole and rises to the third post, allowing the workpiece to be tucked under the back pole while resting on the front pole. The rise in height of the back pole and the horizontal divergence means that pieces of widely different shape and size can be held on a brake.

If it is an advantage to be able to move your brake it can be made from a pallet and pieces of scrap 4 x 4in and 4 x 2in. A brake is virtually essential for effective green woodworking.

Hand Tools

'There's always another way!' Fortunately Windsor chairmaking is relatively low tech, and most operations can be undertaken in several different ways. For example, hollowing the seat can be done with adze, inshave and travisher. You could do without the inshave quite easily, and you needn't buy an adze if you have plenty of time to do all the hollowing with the travisher. This would be hard work on your thumbs, but quite feasible if the wood is not too hard.

If you don't wish to buy any of these tools, then the seat could be hollowed with a mallet and gouge only. Both of these will be needed elsewhere in making the chair, so they would be useful (if not essential) purchases, but the hollowing would take considerably more time and effort than if you began with the three tools that were specialized for the job. If money is limited, then buy the minimum and upgrade gradually to specialized tools that will make specific tasks easier and more efficient.

Splitting Tools

A sledgehammer is essential for splitting large pieces of wood. It does not need to be large – a 7lb head is quite sufficient – and it may be worth shortening the handle so that the overall length of the hammer is only approximately 22in (55cm).

At least three metal wedges are needed. Make sure that they taper gently to the edge. If the taper is too steep the wedge will never bite, and will bounce out of the wood after each hammer blow. Large wooden wedges can be fashioned on the bandsaw, or even with a chainsaw, to open up logs that have been split but which are still held together by large fibres of wood running across the split.

Once the large sections of wood have been split with wedges, more delicate splitting can be undertaken with a froe. This tool has a blade with a handle at right angles. The blade is first hammered with a wooden club into the end grain of the wood to be split, then by twisting the blade about its length with the handle the two halves are moved apart, extending the split along the length of the wood. The blade does not need to be particularly sharp because it is a splitting rather than a cutting tool.

Splitting tools: sledge hammer, steel wedge, club, froe.

Drawknife

This tool is perfectly described by its name. The blade should be sharpened like a knife, with a bevel on both sides; it is then drawn through the wood by pulling on the handles. There are many styles of drawknife on the market, some good and others not worth considering.

For instance, do not purchase a knife with a straight blade with a bevel ground just on one side. If it is used to smooth a wide piece of wood, then the straightness of the blade will mean that it will cut over the full width of the wood – which may not be desirable, or even possible to pull if it is too wide. A curved blade reduces the cutting width for light cuts, and also encourages a slicing action which helps the blade move through the wood. A single bevel, which is often ground on the top of the blade, will act like a chisel. Once it begins to bite into the wood it will tend to go ever deeper, and be nearly impossible to steer back to the surface during the cut.

The blade should ideally have been forged, rather than cut out of a piece of bar, and be relatively thin. The bevel on the top surface should be slightly steeper than the lower bevel, but both should be rounded as opposed to hollow ground. This type of blade can be moved in and out of the wood at will, and will afford great control when shaving thin pieces of wood such as spindles.

Spokeshaves

This tool is less aggressive and more controllable than the drawknife, and should be used only after as much wood as possible has been removed by the drawknife. On dry wood, however, it may be the first tool to be used.

Wooden spokeshaves with their blades held at a low angle to the wood are perfect for green woodworking and chairmaking. With the soft green wood large amounts can be removed very quickly, while delicate cuts can also be made to produce a fine surface. Holding the tool with the fingertips around the blade gives the best 'feel' for what is happening at the blade. The handles of most shaves are for decoration and should not be used.

Inexpensive metal shaves rarely work well and in my opinion have no place in a chairmaker's workshop. One or two good quality wooden spokeshaves are absolutely essential for successful chairmaking, and should be considered the equivalent of the cabinetmaker's planes.

The use of the wooden spokeshave has been largely forgotten with the rise in use of power tools, and the best way to use them is not always obvious. It is most important that a light grip is kept on the tool, around the blade, and that the body of the tool directly in front of the blade is kept in contact with the wood at all times. Concentrate on this contact, and imagine the blade being trailed along lightly behind it. Using this method both light and heavy cuts can be made with the blade on a relatively coarse setting.

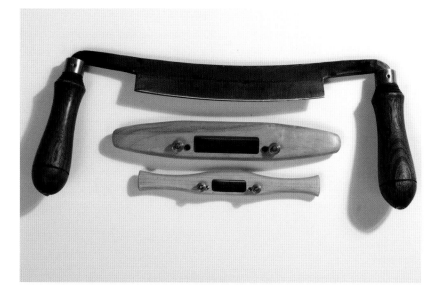

Shaving tools: drawknife, and spokeshaves made by the author.

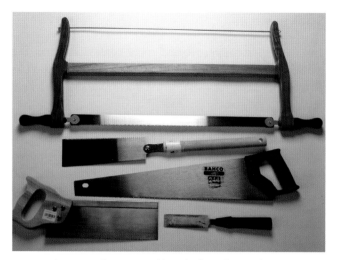

A range of saws used in Windsor chairmaking.

Hollowing tools: adze, scorp (inshave), travisher.

MAKING SPOKESHAVES

When I began to make chairs, the importance of the wooden spokeshave soon became apparent. It was difficult to find well designed new tools, and old shaves tend to be worn in the blade, body or tang holes. I decided to make my own shaves, and saw it as an opportunity to modify the traditional design and make tools better suited for making chairs.

The traditional design has a number of weaknesses. First, the handles are designed for pushing the tool. Pulling is possible, but it tends to be done in spite of the handles, rather than assisted by them. I decided to do away with distinct handles so that the hands of the user grip the body directly in front of and behind the blade, giving maximum feedback from the blade.

The back of the traditional body is cut out (to allow the escape of shavings) in precisely the place that the thumbs should be for pushing the tool. My design allows the shavings to come out of the top of the tool, leaving a continuous wooden surface for pushing with the thumbs – and also for fingers when pulling. The continuous back also supports the back of the blade along its whole length, reducing the tendency for chatter.

Old shaves had a friction fit of the blade into the body. However, this wears in time so that it is difficult to adjust the blade precisely. This arrangement has been replaced with holes for the threaded posts of the blades, and grub screws for adjustment. The blades are pulled up on to the adjustable screws.

Saws

Sawing in chairmaking is mainly done to trim pieces to length. Joints in Windsor chairs are not made with saws so they don't have to be particularly sophisticated, but a range is useful:

- A bowsaw with coarse teeth is good for cutting wet logs, although it may be quicker to use a chainsaw (if you have neighbours, an electric chainsaw might be considered less noisy).
- A frame saw with a narrow blade can be used to cut out seat blanks.
- A hard-point carpenter's saw is always useful; it cross-cuts green wood very effectively.
- Japanese pull-saws cut very cleanly and are probably more useful than tenon saws. A large and a small version would be useful.
- Finally, through tenons need to be trimmed as flush as possible with a saw. Specialist flush-cutting saws – normally used for trimming dowels and plugs – are available, and work very well, but a small Japanese flexible saw might do the job as well.

Travisher – a curved spokeshave designed for hollowing seats. This design was developed by the author along the same lines as the wooden spokeshaves on page 45.

Power hollowing: the Arbotech blade on the angle grinder eliminates the effort of using an adze.

Hollowing Tools

ADZE

A curved adze is perfect for hollowing a seat. Often known as a guttering adze, it will remove chips aggressively, and with practice can produce a fairly smooth surface that needs little work with a travisher. Personally I prefer a long-handled adze, used standing up between the feet. Others favour hand adzes, but the larger adze tends to be more aggressive and you can work more quickly with it. This is potentially one of the most dangerous tools to use, and its safe use will be considered in the next chapter.

New adzes will almost all require a degree of regrinding to produce a small slightly rounded bevel on the outside of the blade. This will allow it to enter and exit the wood cleanly, leaving a smooth scalloped cut. Achieving the ideal angle between wood and blade is the most important part of successful adzing.

SCORP

This is a curved drawknife and was traditionally used after the adze for clean-up and further wood removal. If you have a good travisher then this tool is almost redundant, but the same comments about blade shape apply to this tool as to the drawknife and adze.

TRAVISHER

A curved wooden spokeshave used only to hollow wooden seats. A broad and deep nose in front of the blade allows great control when hollowing a seat. Often the tool works better across the grain, and if the grain is wild you will need to hunt for an appropriate direction that does not tear the grain.

This tool is capable of both coarse and fine cuts, and minimal scraping should be necessary after its use. This is one of the most enjoyable tools to use and is highly recommended.

Arbortech

This circular blade fitted to an angle grinder can take the place of the adze. With careful use, it is extremely effective in shaping seats, but it is noisy and creates a lot of mess over a wide area. Full protective clothing (face mask, ear defenders, dust mask, gloves, sleeves) should be worn, otherwise it is a most unpleasant and unsafe experience. If a single seat is to be shaped then hand tools will be just as quick (minimal set-up time), but if a set of chairs is being made, then the tool is a great addition to the workshop.

Rasps: a very coarse rasp for rapid stock removal, and hand-cut rasps for finer work.

Cabinet scrapers: the best value tool in the workshop if you can sharpen them.

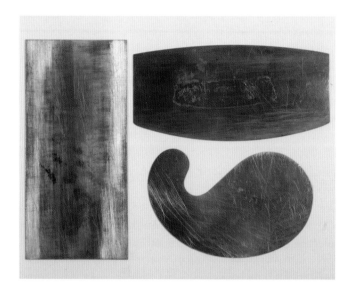

Sharpening a scraper: a) File off any existing bur, keeping the file absolutely flat.

b) Grind a bevel (approximately 45 degrees) using a belt sander.

It is capable of very fine work when held appropriately. In my early years as a chairmaker I used to trim the tops of the leg tenons with one after they had been glued and wedged in the finished seat. One slip would have ruined many hours of work, but it never happened!

Rasps

For shaping hardwood seats rasps can be excellent when used in conjunction with spokeshaves. A rasp can remove wood (particularly end grain) very quickly and accurately, while a finely set spokeshave will finish off the surface.

A machine-made rasp is highly aggressive and is excellent for stock removal, while hand-cut rasps create a superb finish which can be cleaned up quickly with a cabinet scraper. A cabinet maker's rasp is perfect for concave surfaces such as on the underside of a bow-back chair seat.

Scrapers

The least expensive, but one of the most effective tools in the workshop – provided it can be effectively sharpened. Both a curved and a straight scraper are essential to chairmaking.

SHARPENING A SCRAPER

This is a quick and effective method for producing an aggressive bur on a scraper for cleaning up a workpiece before sanding.

Create a bevel on one side of the scraper using a file, or more quickly a belt sander (100–120 grit). This process in itself generates a bur, but it has no strength. Next hold the scraper flat on the bench within an inch of the edge, with the bevel down. Take a burnisher, and angling it just up from the horizontal, rub back and forth along the back of the bevel exerting considerable downward pressure. This is a very important stage as you are removing the first bur and work-hardening the edge. Once you feel the amount of friction increase, stop. Place the scraper in a vice with approximately 1in (2.5cm) protruding, with the bevel facing into the bench. Hold one end of the burnisher on the bench, and the handle in the other hand. With firm pressure down on to the edge, push the burnisher along the edge. One pass should produce a visible and most effective edge.

To resharpen, hold the scraper flat on the bench and file off the bur (taking care to keep the file flat). Then regrind the bevel before creating the bur. It is easy to sharpen gooseneck scrapers this way, particularly if the bevel is ground freehand on a belt sander. For a curved scraper hold it in the vice with the bevel facing out from the bench. Otherwise the process is identical.

c) Prepare the edge by rubbing it hard with the bevel down.

d) Create the bur: hold the scraper in the vice (bevel facing into the bench) and run the burnisher along the edge at an angle, keeping the end in contact with the bench for safety.

Abrasives

Abrasives should be used by chairmakers as little as possible to minimize dust. Sanding can also waste enormous amounts of time, which would not be necessary if a better finish had been produced prior to sanding. Cloth-backed abrasives, although expensive, are the most economical choice. Three pieces (120, 180 and 240 grit) approximately 150 x 100mm should be plenty for a complete chair. One major advantage of cloth-backed abrasive is that it can be used wet for sanding on the lathe without any deterioration.

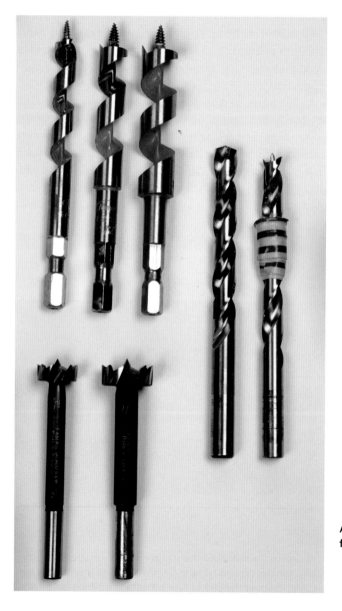

Drills and Bits

A bow-back chair has twenty-six holes and a sack-back has forty-five. Drilling holes is a major part of making a chair, and selecting the best bit will make the job easier.

Forstner bits: These are ideal for drilling the major holes in the seat with a pillar drill. They cut clean holes and will enter the wood at an angle without skidding sideways. When the smaller sizes are used to drill deep holes through seats there is a tendency for them to become clogged with shavings. If this is not avoided by clearing the bit (lift the bit now and again, though not necessarily all the way out of the hole) the cutting edges will heat up and lose their temper ruining the bit. These are expensive, but if well looked after will prove good value.
Auger bits: Short-pattern bits that can be used in a brace or a cordless drill. The long screw point draws the bit into the wood allowing holes to be drilled at angles. This is a great advantage when drilling through a bow for one of the outer spindles. Keep the cutting edge sharp to avoid tear-out when using the larger sizes at an angle. The deeply hollowed shank allows waste to move up the drill, and clearing the bit should not be necessary during drilling. Sometimes these bits produce holes slightly larger than stated on the drill. This is not a problem in Windsor chair making provided it is known about, as the tenons are all made over-size (*see* Chapter 3).
Twist drills: These general purpose bits can be used for undemanding tasks such as making depth-holes in the seat.
Lip and spur bits: With a significant leading point these will not wander like round-nosed bits, but they will tend to tear wood badly if introduced to it at any angle other than 90 degrees.

A range of drill bits: auger, forstner, brad point, twist drill.

Hammers

A range of hammers is used to make a chair. I do not use a mallet, but prefer a nylon-shafted hammer with replaceable heads, opting for one hard and the other soft.

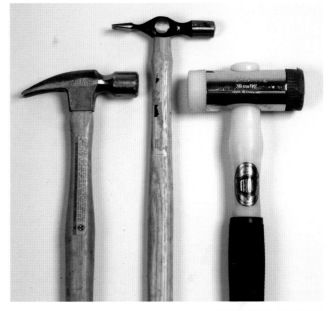

A range of hammers useful for Windsor chairmaking. The plastic hammer with the hard and soft face is more versatile than a mallet.

MINIMUM TOOL LIST FOR MAKING WINDSOR CHAIRS

Bandsaw (not absolutely essential but highly recommended – use bowsaw for cutting out seats as an alternative)	Pillar drill and tilting table (not absolutely essential but highly recommended)	Lathe
Froe	Club	Spirit level
Hand saws	Adze	Bevel gauge
Hammers	Rasp	Square
24in rule	Roughing gouge (3/4")	Protractor
Speed clamps	Parting tool	Drawknife
Drill bits (imperial):	Skew chisel	Spokeshaves (medium and small)
Forstner: $\frac{7}{8}$, $\frac{11}{16}$, $\frac{5}{8}$	Callipers (x 5)	Travisher
Auger: $\frac{5}{8}$, $\frac{1}{2}$, $\frac{3}{8}$	Brace	Sledge hammer
Drill bits (metric):	Cordless drill (say, 14v)	Splitting wedges (2–3)
10.5mm, 11.5mm	Cabinet scrapers	Froe
	Burnisher	

CHAPTER 3

PROCESSES AND TECHNIQUES

Steam-bending

Steam-bending is a process that all woodworkers should try at some point in their lives. It is possible to make Windsors without steam-bending, but in most cases it is simpler and quicker than the alternative of laminating.

Two elements are needed to steam-bend wood successfully: heat and moisture. The moisture comes from inside the wood, and the steam raises its temperature to approximately 100°C and prevents the wood from drying out too much in the process. The same conditions could be achieved by boiling the wood in water, but practical considerations make this a more cumbersome and energy-intensive process. Ash, oak and sweet chestnut all bend well, and it is worth trying other hardwoods if these are not readily available, or you wish to use different woods.

Although in this chapter only the use of green wood split from a tree is considered, this is not the only source of materials. Straight-grained, sawn, air-dried wood will work, particularly if the wood has not been dried for too long. The risk of using sawn wood is that unless it is very straight there will be short grain at some point along the bow, which may lead to failure. Do not try to bend kiln-dried wood (unless you are desperate) as it has been cooked and the character of the wood has been altered, which will result in a much higher failure rate.

The first priority is to find wood that has straight grain and no knots. Small knots may be acceptable in turnings, but they will have an effect disproportionate to their size when the wood is bent.

STEERING THE SPLIT

When splitting wood it is important that the split runs along the grain lines (growth rings and medullary rays) and does not cross them, otherwise wood will be wasted because the final piece must have continuity of grain over its entire length.

The split should be started with equal amounts of wood on either side of the split. In reality the wood on each side must be equally stiff for the split to run true, but this can be approximated to equal surface areas on each side. However, even with the greatest care the split may tend to wander over the length of the wood, and it is important to be able to steer the split back on track if you are not to waste large amounts of wood. To steer the split, place the froe as close to the start of the split as possible, and, holding the piece in a brake, put pressure on the whole piece in the direction in which you want the split to move. While applying the pressure, twist the froe with the handle and closely watch the movement of the split. When it has moved back to the ideal line, release the pressure and continue with the froe alone. If it wanders again, repeat the process. This is a technique that can only be truly understood by practice, as the amount of pressure required will vary from piece to piece and species to species.

The following equipment will be required for bending an arm or bow:

- a former
- a bending strap - ideally made of stainless steel
- pegs and wedges
- a steam box and source of steam

Preparation of blank prior to bending

There are alternative methods of preparing green wood for bending and I will share two with you. The first involves only hand tools, while the second uses a bandsaw to reduce the physical effort required. If you plan to make just one bow then the first method will work well; but bending is not always successful and I prefer to make several bends in a session to guarantee myself at least one good bend and hopefully have some spares for the next time.

METHOD 1 (HAND TOOLS ONLY)
Cut the wood to length. Let us assume you have a quarter-round at this stage, perhaps with a radius of 4-5in. Split it once

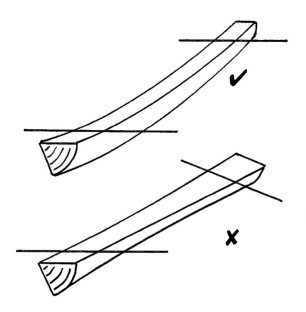

If wood is curved along its length it can still be used for bending, but try to avoid wood that twists along its length.

more into ⅛-round using a wedge and sledge hammer.

This sized piece can then be transferred to a brake for further splitting with a froe. The aim is to split it into a piece that is as close to the final size as possible, with all the split surfaces running with (and not across) the grain of the wood.

The split piece should now be studied to find the two surfaces that can most easily be made at 90 degrees to each other. The wood may not be straight, but this is not important as it is going to be bent, and the existing curve can determine the direction in which to bend it. Concentrate on maintaining the 90 degree angle over the full length, and not crossing grain lines. The drawknife is the tool of choice for this process, and fine-tuning can be done with a spokeshave.

Once the two faces have been shaved flat and are at 90 degrees to each other, mark the required width on these faces with a pencil. Drawknife down to these marks on both sides, creating the two other faces also at right angles. The bow is then ready for bending.

In producing a bow using this method the original wood has to be split before the drawknife can be used. Since the blank needs to be larger than the final size, there will be waste for each bow produced. The amount of waste depends on the accuracy of splitting, but it can be considerable. The second method, using a bandsaw minimizes the waste, and the physical effort required.

METHOD 2 (BANDSAW)
Starting with a quarter-round (as described above), use a drawknife to flatten the better of the two faces. As before, the face may be curved but it should not be twisted along its length; and the face should not deviate from a radial plane. The object of this exercise is to use the bandsaw to make cuts in line with the grain of the wood instead of splitting along the grain. If care is not taken to cut along the grain then the key benefit of using split green wood is lost, and you would be better off buying sawn wood from a mill and just cutting in a straight line, whether or not it crosses the grain.

If the bark is removed from the edge of the prepared face this provides a surface that runs perfectly in line with the annual rings of the tree. If this edge is run along a fence the band saw will make cuts that are also perfectly along the annual rings. A point fence is required in this case because the piece may be curved and all that is required is a constant gap between the fence and the blade. With practice it is very easy to make parallel cuts in curved wood in this way.

Once the first cut has been made, then a sequence of cuts will produce blanks ready for bending (see diagram).

The size of the piece of wood to be sawn will depend entirely on the size and power of your bandsaw, and the weight of wood that you can comfortably handle. The benefits of perfecting this technique are speed, minimum physical effort, and minimum wastage.

There is no need to clean up bandsaw marks on the wood before bending; although the surface is rough it will not lead to failure. Steam-bending is not a guaranteed process and failures do happen, and sometimes for inexplicable reasons. Therefore it is wise to invest as little effort as possible in the wood prior to bending. Once it has been successfully bent (and dried), then you should lavish care on it.

A bending strap will increase the success rate considerably because it will support the outer surface of the wood as it is being bent. The outside surface will tend to stretch while the inner surface compresses. Wood can accept far more compression than tension without failing, so minimizing or eliminating stretching on the outside is a good thing.

Fit blocks to the ends of the strap, which will compress the ends of the wood as it is being bent. Cut the wood to fit between the blocks with a slight inward taper so that all the compression from the blocks is first directed to the outside surface. On a long bend a slight gap (say, ⅛in/3mm) is desirable between the ends of the wood and the end blocks. It will make fitting the hot bow to the strap easier, and the gap will quickly close as the wood is bent. Mark the centre of the wood with a large arrow to show the centre and therefore the orientation when it comes out of the steam box.

Steam the blank in the steam box for the necessary length of time, carefully remove it (taking care of the steam on hands

Point fence clamped to the table of the bandsaw. Note the bark shaved off adjacent to the fence, giving an edge parallel to the growth rings.

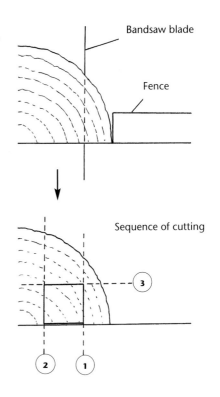

A point fence is ideal for creating a strip of wood of constant thickness even if it is curved along its length.

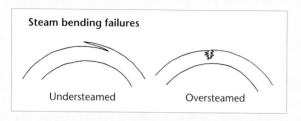

Steam bending failures

Understeamed   Oversteamed

Wood tends to delaminate if it has been understeamed, and to break across the grain if it has been oversteamed.

HOW LONG TO STEAM FOR?

The answer is more art than science. If you are able to keep most of the variables constant (as in an industrial process), then trial and error will give a suitable time and it should never vary. However, working on a small scale, and bending wood occasionally, it is difficult to keep everything the same.

Given that you have sufficient steam, and the temperature in the box is very close to 100°C, the moisture content of the wood and the species to be bent will have the greatest impact on the timing. The general rule of thumb is that one hour's steaming is necessary for 1in (2.5cm) of dry wood (say, 12 per cent), whereas green wood will need half the time. A moisture content of 18 per cent is considered optimal for bending. If a piece of ash requires thirty minutes of steaming to bend, then the same dimension in oak may only require ten minutes.

Trial and error are the best guides, but it can be a frustrating process. It is just as possible to over-steam as to under-steam, and characteristic failures will result: thus under-steaming will lead to delamination, while over-steaming will cause the fibres to fail across the piece, leaving a ragged fracture. Small delaminations can be glued back together, but other failures should be discarded immediately.

and condensation on glasses) and fit it between the blocks on the strap. Align the centre mark with the centre of the former, clamp it to the former using a wedge, and steadily bend the wood all the way round. Secure it in place with a peg and wedge. If you use a winch, then both arms of the bow will be bent at the same time, but it is perfectly acceptable to bend one arm at a time.

The bend is not set until the wood has dried, so it is important to tie the ends of the bow together a few minutes after bending so that the jig can be readied for the next bend. If it slips off the former before being tied, it will immediately begin to unbend and will need to be discarded. Dry the bend before

Bending–jig ready to bend an arm. The winch pulls both ends of the arm at once with minimum effort.

The arm after bending, held in place with pegs and wedges.

Alternative blocks at the end of the strap, which compress the end of the wood being bent.

ASH AND OAK

Ash is a more dependable bending wood than oak, particularly if it has dried out somewhat from its felled state. However, oak's colour, grain patterns and ease of working make it worth the inevitable failures on the way to success.

Fresh, straight-grained English oak is a superb wood for bending. In my experience it will not bend to such a tight radius as ash, but for virtually all circumstances in Windsor chairmaking it is excellent. However, after approximately three months of storage under a sheet (to prevent moisture loss) its bendability becomes very poor, and failures similar to those from over-steaming become common. This is due to fungal weakening of the wood, promoted by conditions of 100 per cent humidity. After this time the wood should be abandoned and a fresh supply found. The period of use is temperature dependent, and oak therefore has a longer shelf life during the cold winter months than in the summer.

cleaning up the surfaces. You will know when it is dry because the string will become loose, indicating that the bend has become tighter.

Bending formers can be made easily from 18mm sheathing ply. Small dimensions will need only one thickness, and further layers can be added for thicker bends. Make formers exactly the shape and size as required for the design, and don't worry about 'spring-back'. This feature is of serious concern to those who laminate curved pieces that must retain a precise shape. Steam bending for Windsor chairs is not such a precise operation, however, and if there is a little spring-back it is rarely the end of the world. A bow can be bent inwards a little to make it fit into the mortices in the seat, and if a crest springs back slightly then the spindles will still fit.

The main reason to ignore spring-back is that with steam-bending it can be controlled, and one can even produce the opposite effect, of spring-forward! Once the wood has been bent around the former it will spring back to close to its original shape if released, but as it dries so the 'released position' will become closer to that of the former. This process continues with drying, so if the bend is over-dried it may become tighter than the former.

If a bow has become too tight, then wrap a damp cloth around the bent part, and use a spreader to separate the ends by the desired distance, and leave it overnight. The bend will unwind in that time, hopefully by the desired amount. If not, then further drying or wetting will sort out the problem.

Preparation of Bent Parts

Pieces that have been steam-bent will need to be cleaned up before they can be incorporated into the chair. Surfaces may have bandsaw marks and other irregularities that you wish to remove, and edges will need to be softened and sometimes rounded over.

The cabinet scraper is the best tool for beginning this job; if it is sharp and used with determination it will clean up these surfaces very quickly. Hold the piece firmly in the vice or on the bench, and scrape. When cleaning up saw marks, angle the scraper so that it cuts the tops of many marks at the same time. This will avoid resonance and eliminate the potential risk of making the surface worse rather than better.

Once scraped, then abrasives can be used to produce the final surface (120, 180 and 240 grit). Alternatively a drum sander, mounted in a pillar drill and with good dust extraction, will speed up the process even further. Starting with 40 grit may eliminate the need for a scraper, though use this coarse abrasive sparingly otherwise your bows and crests may lose too much wood.

The drum sander is excellent at rounding over edges and speedily producing a fine surface.

Making the Parts

Turning

Turning is a discipline in its own right. I am assuming familiarity with the lathe, but will consider techniques to achieve sets of pieces, such as legs, for inclusion in the chair. Turning green wood is a real pleasure when compared with dry wood. There is no dust and the wood is much softer and easier to shape, and with practice parts can be replicated quickly – I aim for four and a half to six minutes per leg, depending on the turning pattern.

Cut the wood to the required length (perhaps 1½in (4cm) longer than the final leg) and split it with a wedge or froe into suitable sized pieces. Any sharp edges, such as the pith on the innermost blank, can be removed with the froe. If the wood is straight, then 2in (5cm) square should be sufficient for 1⅝– 1¾in diameter legs.

Holding the wood in the vice, remove the remaining sharp edges with a drawknife and create a blank that is closer to round than square. The primary reason for this step is safety. When an irregularly shaped piece of wood is spun at up to 2,000rpm, the more irregular the surface, the greater the risk of the gouge jamming, and causing the piece to break away from the lathe, with unpleasant results.

Finally, carefully balance it between the lathe's centres, and secure it tightly with the tailstock.

Create cylinders, whose diameters correspond to key points on the turning, before shaping.

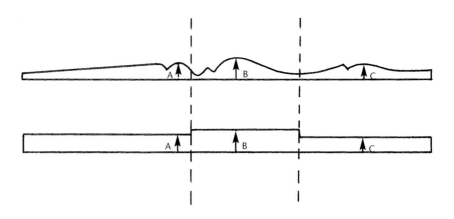

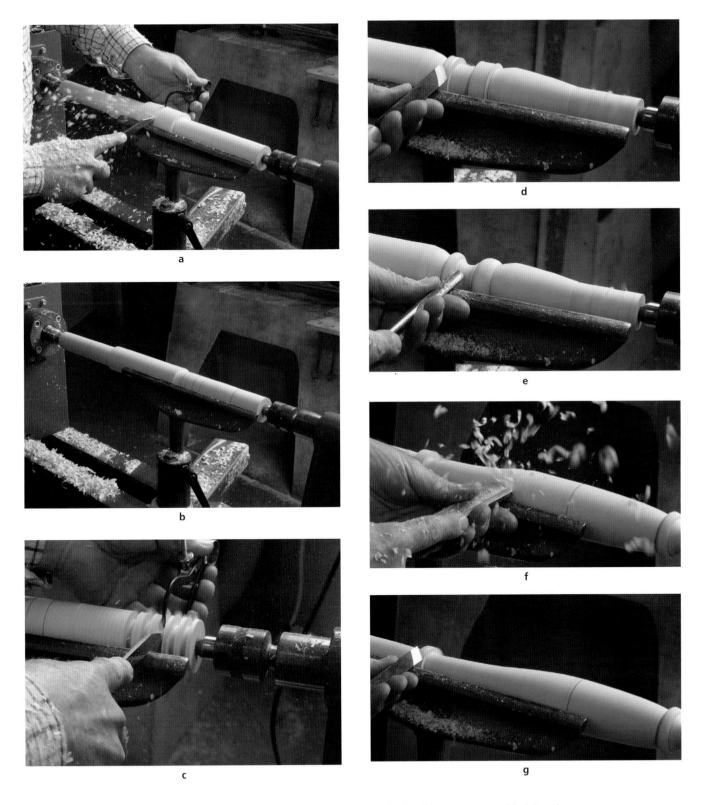

Making an English leg: (a) forming a three-step cylinder; (b) marking out; (c) sizing the tenon;
(d)–(g) forming the details and creating the main shape.

BALANCING A TURNING BLANK

If the blank has been produced by splitting, then it will have an irregular shape. If it is not balanced on the lathe there will be vibration when it is spun, and if this is too severe the piece could tear itself off the lathe and injure the turner or someone watching.

With care, even the most irregular piece can be accurately balanced. First, place the tip of the drive as close as possible to the centre of one end of the blank. Next advance the tip of the tailstock, and centre it again by eye. The piece should now be held by two points and be free to rotate. Spin it by hand and notice whether it always stops in the same orientation. If it does then it is not balanced, and there it too much weight below the tailstock. Release the tailstock, raise the piece, and grip it again with the point. Respin the blank and repeat the process until it is accurately balanced and it settles in different orientations each time.

Reduce the blank to a cylinder using a ¾in roughing gouge. Work very gently to start with, and increase the pressure as the surface becomes smoother. Do not measure the cylinder at this stage, as long as you keep it larger than the maximum

diameter of the leg. Make sure that the rest is at an appropriate height so that the gouge is peeling the wood from the surface rather than scraping it off.

To replicate pieces quickly and accurately it is important to develop a systematic approach that is followed time and again until it becomes second nature. Once one ceases to have to think about the order of working, and can concentrate on shaping the wood, then your speed will increase significantly.

Look at the pattern to be turned and reduce it to two or perhaps three lengths all of the same diameter – see the examples. The diameters will coincide with the high points of the turning pattern. Mark a stick with the transition points, and transfer them to the spinning blank with a pencil. Then size the cylinders using a parting tool and callipers (a maximum of three sizings per cylinder) and remove the excess with the gouge. Mark on all the key measurements, and size them with the parting tool and callipers.

As a general principle, size as few points as possible and rely on your turning to produce similar shapes each time between these points. Sizing takes time, and with a little repetition the shapes produced will become more and more similar. If your turnings are a little variable to begin with, then it is helpful to remember that the human eye finds it very difficult to compare two or more legs critically when they are in a chair at angles to each other.

The tenon should be left oversize to allow for shrinkage during drying. For a ⅞in dry tenon, create the wet tenon of approximately 1 1/16in diameter. If you are copying a leg from an existing chair, then add 1/16in (1.6mm) to each measurement to take account of the green wood shrinking and for losses during sanding.

My personal experience suggests that it is not necessary to use a skew chisel to create flat and tapering surfaces. I prefer to maximize the use of the roughing gouge and to use abrasives to clean up the resulting small ridges. Others will be determined to create a planed surface all over the piece, particularly if using a pole lathe.

Although not conventional, sanding your completed turning before drying is quick, effective, and produces absolutely no dust. Cloth-backed abrasive, a pad, a small sponge and a bucket of water are all that are required.

First remove the tool rest, and with the lathe running, wet the sponge and run it along the workpiece to moisten it. Wet the abrasive by dipping it in the bucket, and with the sponge held in your left hand and the abrasive on the pad in your right

---

SPEED OF TURNING

Speed of turning comes from confidence and technique (which will only develop with time), but also from minimizing movements and changes of tool. If possible set up a tool rack immediately behind the workpiece to hold your chisels and callipers. You should be able to see which tool is which at a glance – replacing the standard handles with different shapes may help. Similarly with callipers (you will probably need five pairs): they should be straight in front of you and clearly labelled, and preferably arranged in the same order that they will be used along the piece to be turned. This type of set-up will minimize the time taken to change tools, and there will be no need to move your body, only your arm. The hour or so that it will take to install such a rack will be repaid many times over the years.

Wet sanding: keep the workpiece wet by squeezing the sponge so that a slurry is formed and the abrasive doesn't clog.

Wet sanding kit: bucket, sponge, foam pad and cloth-backed abrasive.

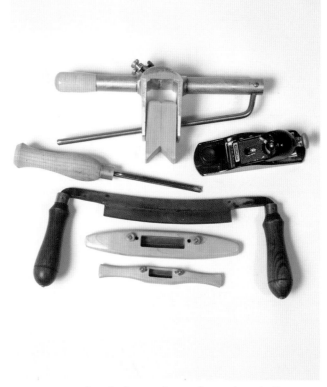

A range of tools that can be used to make spindles.

hand, run them back and forth along the piece. Make sure that the abrasive never dries out by constantly adding water by squeezing the sponge. A slurry will be created, and if there is sufficient water the abrasive will not clog. When you have finished with the first grit (I suggest 120, 180 and 240 grits), rinse off the abrasive and repeat the process with the next grit. Repeat until the three grits have been used.

At this stage the piece can be put to dry. Oak that has been wet-sanded will be much less prone to splitting than unsanded wood, as the sawdust slurry will have blocked the pores of the wood, slowing down the drying process.

Making the Spindles

Spindles in a Windsor catch the eye, and many people believe that they are a defining feature of these chairs; therefore making them attractive is crucial to the visual success of the chair. Ugly spindles will perform their structural job as well as elegant ones, but who wants to make ugly chairs?

There are several ways to make spindles, but in general American spindles are shaved while English spindles are turned. Turning can be done at high speed with a small bowl gouge followed by a block plane, or at a slow speed using a trapping plane. As with the whole chair, elegance is the quality that should be aimed for in a spindle: this means leaving no unnecessary wood in the spindle, and making smooth changes in diameter along its length. Look at eighteenth-century chairs and you will rarely find heavy spindles – in England or America. Engineering perfection is definitely not a requirement: look at a machine-made spindle which is perfectly smooth and round, and it will appear lifeless. Spindles in old chairs often have kinks and irregularities arising from the wood and tools that were used, but these are positive features that give the chair character. When making spindles aim for perfec-

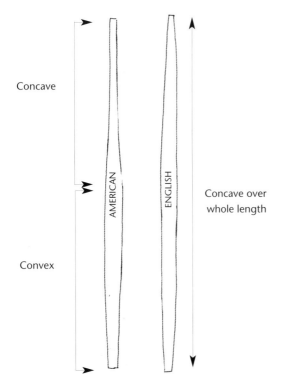

Concave

Convex

AMERICAN

ENGLISH

Concave over whole length

American spindles usually have both convex and concave tapers; while English spindles are usually convex along their full length.

Steering the split: the blank is held in the open vice, using it as a brake, and the whole blank is pulled towards the author while the froe is twisted, to move the split towards the author.

Creating spindle blanks with the froe.

MIXING IMPERIAL AND METRIC MEASUREMENTS

Just occasionally it may be sensible to mix units. A ⅝in hole will leave plenty of wood to create a ½in diameter tenon when dry; and a 10.5mm hole is just larger than the ⅜in (9.5mm) hole that will be drilled in the bow. When the spindle dries, the wet 10.5mm tenon will shrink close to ⅜in and require very little adjustment. You are unlikely to have a $^{13}/_{32}$in drill, but a 10.5mm drill may be available. $^{7}/_{16}$in would be unnecessarily large. Hence the mixing of units.

tion and the character will enter by itself. Try to add character, and you will get too much!

SPINDLE SHAPE

The shape of English and American spindles is different, in part due to the way that they are fitted into the bow. English spindles are almost always blind-tenoned, while most American spindles pass through the bow and are then glued and wedged.

The most significant difference between the two traditions, apart from the way in which they are made, is that American spindles frequently have a concave taper towards the top, while English spindles are concave along their full length. The difference is subtle, but the presence of convex curves is also much more common in other parts of American chairs, such as leg turnings. English spindles in the eighteenth century were made over-size at the top, and then trimmed to fit into a blind mortice in the arm or bow. This trimming was often done with a gouge from approximately ½in (12mm) below the bow, and often on just one side of the spindle.

If you study the base of spindles in old chairs (English and American) you will usually find flats where the spindle has been faceted with a drawknife, and then driven oversize into the hole in the seat.

PREPARATION OF SPINDLE BLANKS

Blanks for oak spindles can be split close to the required size. The blanks should be as close to the final size as possible to minimize the amount of wood used and shaping that is needed. Careful use of a froe in straight grained and knot-free wood will quickly produce spindle blanks with the minimum of waste.

Remember to halve the wood each time it is split, and steer the split if it wanders from the desired line. Do your splitting adjacent to some form of brake so that steering the split becomes part of the process. The open jaws of a vice will work well, and you could even improvise with the stretchers of a stool.

Ash spindle blanks are probably better made using a bandsaw. Use straight-grained wood and split the wood into quarters (or less with a big tree). Make one of the two split faces flat using a drawknife or plane, and peel off the bark adjacent to the flat surface, taking care not to remove any of the underlying wood. This edge will run against the fence and ensure

(a) Mark circles top and bottom using gauge.

(b) Shave towards the bottom circle.

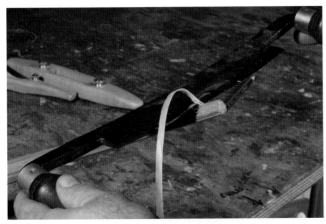

(c) Shave towards the top circle.

(d) Shave the spindle to a pleasing shape.

(e) Size the top tenon with a small spokeshave and gauge.

that the cuts are in line with the grain. ⅞in square blanks are suitable for most spindles.

SHAVING A SPINDLE (WET)

Let us consider the shaving of an American-style bow-back spindle.

Trim the blank to length (allowing some excess at the top). Mark circles on each end using a gauge, ideally made from plastic, with two holes, ⅝in and 10.5mm in diameter.

Hold the top of the spindle in the vice, and shave with the drawknife close to the bottom circle, tapering it from roughly half way along the spindle. Use the drawknife to systematically remove the ridges around the spindle, as this will remove the wood more quickly and take less effort than a multitude of fine cuts. Use a spokeshave to smooth the surface and bring the

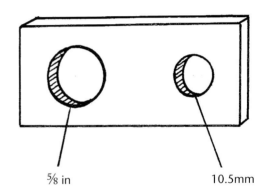

⅝ in   10.5mm

DRAWKNIFING AND SPOKESHAVING

When using the drawknife, hold the spindle either horizontal or sloping up from the bench, at a height that allows your shoulders to be completely relaxed. Spokeshaving is best done vertically so that you can see and work all around the spindle without having to adjust it in the vice.

For shaping the wood, long flowing cuts are ideal with both tools, but once a spokeshave is used for sizing, then the length of cut should be minimized (perhaps maximum 2in/5cm) to avoid taking off wood in the wrong place.

Spindling with a small bowl gouge. Use your hand to support the spinning spindle along as much of its length as possible.

Grind the gouge with a steep angle to give a small cut and help to prevent a 'catch'.

taper to the line of the circle.

Turn the spindle around, holding the (now round) base in the vice, and taper towards the top circle. This tenon needs to be sized accurately, in order to produce a good joint in the bow. Make a long, smooth taper from a point roughly one third up from the base all the way to the top, taking long smooth cuts with the drawknife. When you do not dare remove any more wood with the drawknife, switch to a spokeshave to smooth out the surface.

When the shape is close to perfect, and the top has not yet been shaved tight to the line (10.5mm diameter), change to a small spokeshave and begin sizing the tenon. Use the 10.5mm gauge and test fit the tenon repeatedly. Add graphite from a pencil to the inside of the gauge and this will mark the high points of the tenon that need to be reduced for a good fit. The tenon should be made approximately 2in (5cm) long. The fit should not be 'squeaky' tight, nor should the gauge be loose: an interference fit is ideal.

When the tenon has been formed, a shoulder may be left between the original taper and the tenon. Smooth this out using a spokeshave so that there is no sudden change of diameter anywhere along the spindle.

Not all spindles are the same as those in a side chair. An American sack-back's (double bow) spindle that passes through the arm and up through the bow has a shoulder upon which the arm sits. The shaft above the arm is almost parallel up to the bow. The parallel shaft can be created in the same way that the top tenon was made for the bow-back (with the gauge) – just over a longer distance.

The wet spindles should then be dried.

ENGLISH SPINDLES

The long spindles in an English double bow do not usually have a shoulder, and taper above and below the arm. The spindle needs to be sized to give a good fit where it passes through the arm, and then tapered to an appropriate size for tenoning at each end – say, 9/16in for a 7/16 mortice in the seat, and 7/16in or larger for a 3/8 mortice in the bow.

TURNING SPINDLES

Turning spindles on the lathe should not be undertaken lightly, and is not suitable for American sack-back spindles as they are so fine above the arm (it is possible, but takes great skill).

Sawn spindle blanks are ideal for English spindles. Don't worry if the grain runs out slightly along the spindle's length: if the spindles are turned wet, then small irregularities may develop when they dry, adding interest to the back of the chair. In practice, partial drying of the blanks prior to turning is a good idea because it stiffens up the wood, reducing vibration on the lathe.

Spindling with a block plane: again use the left hand to reduce vibrations. The throat of the plane controls the amount of cut.

Trapping plane: run at about 400rpm; this will remove wood very quickly with minimal vibration.

Mount a blank on the lathe and select a fast speed such as 2,000rpm. Using a small bowl gouge with a steeply ground bevel, remove the corners to such an extent that the left hand can support the spinning spindle while it is being shaped (or remove the corners with drawknife/spokeshaves before mounting on the lathe). The risk of this style of turning is that the spindle will tend to vibrate as it is not very stiff, and it will become impossible to create a smooth surface. If this vibration is allowed to develop unchecked the spindle may come free of the lathe.

With practice it should be possible to remove a considerable amount of wood using the bowl gouge while supporting the spindle with the left hand. Once you feel you are reaching the limit of this process, remove the tool rest and change to a block plane. The wide sole of the plane will help to support the spindle on either side of the cutting edge when used on a skew (you will still need the left hand supporting it as well), and the fully controlled blade will prevent a catch and disaster. Practise running both hands together (with the plane) up and down the spindle. Check key diameters regularly. This method is ideal for English spindles that have to be tenoned by hand at each end.

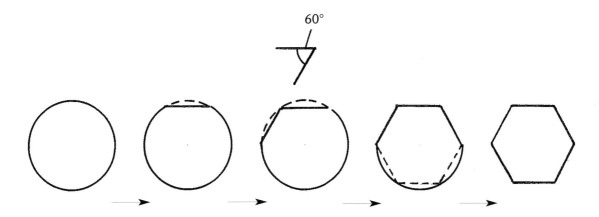

Sequential cuts with a drawknife will form an hexagonal tenon. Each face is 60 degrees from its neighbour.

USING THE TRAPPING PLANE

An alternative to the block plane is the trapping plane that is made for just this purpose. Take your square blank (partially dried) and bevel each edge with a drawknife before mounting on the lathe, which should be set at approximately 400rpm.

Squeeze the trapping plane more towards the ends as you move the tool up and down the blank, regularly checking diameters at the top, middle and bottom of the spindle. A digital set of callipers is ideal for this job as the measurement can be read instantly. Continue the process until the desired dimensions are reached. Allowance should be made for the wood to shrink as it dries fully.

Partially dry wood is softer than fully dry wood, and easier to shape with the trapping plane. Also the shaped and dried surface can be smoothed more easily with abrasives than if dried wood had been used from the beginning.

MAKING THE BOTTOM TENONS

Whether your spindles have been turned or shaved, they will not yet have had their bottom tenons formed. The time to make them is once they are dry and will shrink no more. As with most tasks in Windsor chairmaking, there are many alternative ways of making tenons, but the method most commonly used by early chairmakers was to produce a facetted, oversize tenon with a drawknife or gouge, and drive it into the seat, deforming the round hole around it to produce a very tight fit.

Mark around the tenon approximately 1in from the base. Hold the spindle in the vice with the tenon towards you, and with a sharp drawknife create a facet on the upper surface beginning just behind the line. The facet should be parallel to the axis of the spindle over the last inch of the spindle so that when it is driven into the seat the tenon doesn't act as a wedge tending to split the seat.

Having made the first facet, create facets on either side of the first, at 60 degrees from the horizontal. Then rotate the spindle through 180 degrees so that the first facet is now underneath. Repeat the process to produce the final three facets. You should now have a tenon approximately 1in (2.5cm) long, with the cross-section of a regular hexagon. It will take a little practice to produce even hexagons of the correct size, so work on spare spindles to begin with.

Drill holes in scrap pieces of wood, with the same drill that will be used to make the seat mortices, to act as gauges to test the size of the tenons. Round over each corner of the hexagon

Shaving a hexagonal tenon using a drawknife – six facets at 60 degrees apart.

Testing a tenon over a hole. A small gap between each face and the rim of the hole is ideal.

at the base of the tenon and then hold it against a test hole. The ideal tenon should sit above the hole with a slight gap between each facet and the edge of the hole. When you are satisfied with the (practice) tenon, drive it into the test hole. If it goes in to its full depth, making a tight joint and without splitting the wood around the mortice, then it is the correct size. Patience and judgement are required to make these joints, and the optimum size of tenon will depend partly on the hardness and strength of the seat wood.

This is a specialist technique that will take a little practice to perfect. Initially results will be variable and it will be slow, but once perfected it is quick and highly effective.

Alternative methods use tenon cutters (usually mounted in a drill) that will produce tenons of the desired diameter. However, these are not foolproof as it is quite possible to make tenons that are not in line with the remainder of the spindle; and sharpening and resetting the cutter can lead to considerable variation in the size of the tenon, ranging from loose to too tight.

I prefer the very simple and low-tech drawknife method, which requires a little skill, a sharp tool, and nothing else.

MAKING THE TOP TENONS
These can be made at this stage for American spindles as they will pass through bows or arms. The top tenons for English spindles, and for spindles socketed into crests, will be made when the spindle has been put into the chair.

If the top of the wet spindle were sized with an appropriate sized gauge, then there should be very little work required to size the dry tenon. For example a 10.5mm wet spindle should shrink to almost exactly ⅜in (9.5mm). Use a plastic gauge in the normal way with a small spokeshave to produce accurate top tenons.

CLEANING UP THE SPINDLES
Cleaning up the spindles can be done with a scraper followed by abrasives, but this removes all the tool marks left by the spokeshave and makes for dull spindles. My preference is never to use abrasives on shaved spindles, but to use a finely set, small spokeshave to take very fine cuts leaving a polished but slightly faceted surface that reflects light in an interesting way. This stage allows for any irregularities created with the

Remove the shoulder left after forming the tenon, with a small spokeshave.

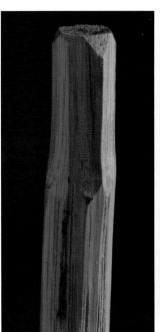

After forming a hexagonal tenon with a drawknife, the remaining shoulder should be removed with a small spokeshave so that the spindle blends into the tenon.

drawknife and larger spokeshave to be smoothed out, and sudden transitions to be eliminated.

Pay particular attention to the bottom of the spindle and blend the body of the spindle down to the hexagonal tenon, removing most of the curved facets made by the drawknife before the cuts became parallel to the spindle.

Making the Seat

The seat is the foundation of the chair, and everything is built out from it. Provided you have chosen a suitable wood of appropriate thickness (1⅜ to 2in/ 4 to 5cm) it will have sufficient strength, and the main challenges will be to drill many holes in it at the correct angles, and to shape it so that it looks and feels good.

CUTTING OUT

The outline shape can be made from a piece of thick cardboard. A half-seat template is ideal so that both sides are guaranteed to be the same. Mark a centre line on the wood and draw round the template to create the shape.

People often ask whether the grain should run across, or from front to back of the seat. This depends on the shape of the seat: if it is roughly square then it doesn't matter – old, square-seated chairs were made with the grain in either direction. However, if the seat is wider than it is deep (for example an American sack back) it is easier to find suitable planks if the grain runs side to side, as they will not need to be so wide. Extra-wide boards should be kept for when their use is absolutely essential, as they are a precious resource. In my opinion side chairs look better if the grain runs from front to back even if they are almost square in shape.

Cut out the blank using the bandsaw. Then run the centre line down each end with a square, and create a centre line on the other side. At this time you should choose which surface will be the top and which the bottom. This decision will depend on the relative attractiveness of the grain, and any imperfections such as knots that you may not want on the visible top surface.

DRILLING THE MAIN HOLES

Before shaping the seat in any way it is good to drill the main holes using a pillar drill. These will be four holes for the legs, and perhaps two holes for a bow, back-posts, or arm-posts. If you wish to drill all the holes in the seat (including those for the spindles) then you will need to know the angle for each spindle and its direction of lean. This is time-consuming to work out accurately for each chair, and it is unnecessary work. It is better to leave drilling these for now.

Drill the main holes before shaping because the shaping may cause the seat to deform, and it will then become more difficult to achieve consistent angles. You must accept that any distortion of the seat will change the actual angles, but hopefully they will remain symmetrical. Stretchers will be made to fit the legs as they stand after shaping (and distortion) so this is not a problem.

It is very unusual to find a hole in a Windsor chair drilled perpendicular to a flat surface, though sometimes they may be drilled perpendicular to a curved surface, but that is another matter. All the holes in the seat will be at an angle from the perpendicular.

SIGHT LINES

I suggest that you forget about the concept of compound angles, where you define an angle as having a component angle to the side (when viewed from the front or back) and a second component angle to the front or back (when viewed

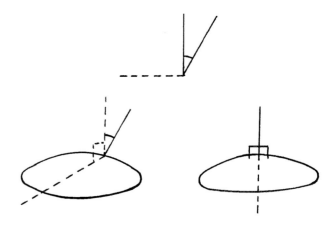

Sight lines show the direction of lean of a component such as a leg. Think of a vertical plane above the line, and the component lying in that plane.

from the side. While this system works when drilling into a flat surface, it becomes meaningless when applied to curved surfaces. Also it is not a very intuitive system to understand.

The direction in which a leg is leaning is known as a sight line. When you look along the sight line at a leg, it will appear to be vertical (a right angle on each side). The leg will lie in a vertical plane above the line, and will lean at a certain angle from the vertical in the plane. The angle from the vertical and the sight line are all that are needed for drilling the hole.

From your plan, mark the positions on the underside of the seat where the drill will enter for each of the leg mortices. Mark on the sight lines, running the line from the point to the edge further away. Write the angle on the seat adjacent to the hole. Repeat this for all the main holes, making sure to mark the holes for the superstructure on the top, and those for the undercarriage on the bottom.

Set up your tilting table on the pillar drill, and adjust it to the correct angle. Place the seat on the table, and bring the drill down to the marked point. While applying gentle pressure to keep the tip of the drill on the mark, rotate the seat around the drill tip until the sight line on the seat is directly above the centre line of the table. The seat will then be in the correct orientation, and the hole can be drilled. Repeat for all the main holes.

Almost all early English Windsors and most American Windsors have leg mortices that pass all the way through the seat. This allows the leg to be glued into the mortice and for a

wedge to be driven into the top to spread the tenon in the mortice and lock it in place. If you wish to drill blind mortices – which do not pass all the way through the seat – then carefully adjust the depth to allow for wood to be removed when shaping the seat without exposing the holes.

MARKING THE SEAT PRIOR TO SHAPING

The first element to mark is the platform for the spindles. This platform is not shaped and the seat remains at its original thickness here. The width of the platform depends on the position of arm-posts, back-posts or bows. The larger holes for these elements need to be surrounded by the platform, since

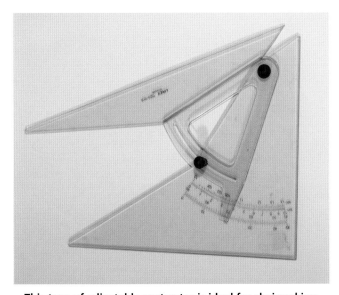

This type of adjustable protractor is ideal for chairmaking.

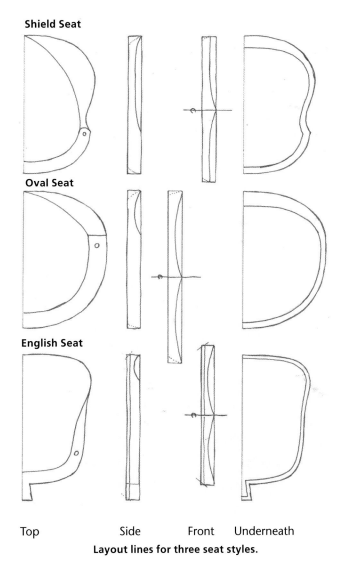

Shield Seat

Oval Seat

English Seat

Top   Side   Front   Underneath

Layout lines for three seat styles.

if the hollowing extends into the hole then some of the tenon will be unattractively exposed. Do not measure the width. Use a finger tip to guide your pencil and run a line around the back of the seat and then smoothly extend the line to the edge of the seat.

Next, mark out the area to be hollowed. This will be bounded by the edge of the spindle platform, and will continue towards the front but in a different pattern, depending on whether an American or English seat is being made.

ENGLISH SEAT HOLLOWING

The whole upper surface of the seat, apart from the spindle platform, is hollowed.

The front legs on English chairs are positioned close to the edge of the seat where there is plenty of wood since the side edges remain at full height on both arm- and side chairs. Hollowing continues all the way to the front edge.

Once the hollowing has been completed, the front edge is shaped so as to give a smooth shape under the thighs of the sitter.

AMERICAN SEAT HOLLOWING

In contrast to English chairs, the front legs penetrate the seat some distance from the edge, and this requires thickness in the seat away from the edge.

A shield-type seat has a roughly circular hollow area between the spindle platform and the front of the seat; however, there are broad convex cheeks on either side of the hollow area which extend from the ends of the spindle platform to the central point at the front.

EDGES – ENGLISH

English chairs are either chamfered on the bottom edge all around the seat, or from just behind the front legs and around the back. This reduces the visual thickness of the seat, although the other seat edges remain vertical. Around the top edge there may be a small bevel, or a bead may be formed.

EDGES – AMERICAN

The edges of an American chair are quite different from those of English chairs. The edge is shaped all around the seat, and nothing remains vertical.

The front edge of these seats is brought to a crisp line by bevelling the underside to meet the convex upper cheeks. This has the effect of reducing the visual thickness of the seat to a line when seen from most directions. By contrast the back of the seat is rounded over to reduce the apparent thickness while retaining the appearance (and reality) of sufficient strength.

Most of this edge shaping can be achieved with a drawknife when soft woods such as pine are used, but hardwoods will require the use of spokeshaves and rasps.

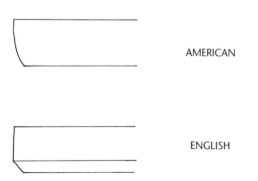

AMERICAN

ENGLISH

Some profiles are more attractive than others. A tapering curve is more attractive than a quarter-round with a vertical face.

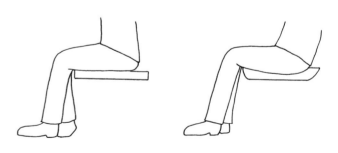

Hollowing a seat spreads the weight of the sitter over a greater surface area reducing the pressure on the skin, and making it more comfortable over an extended period.

SEAT COMFORT

If you sit on a flat plank of wood, it may be comfortable for a while because it relieves the body's weight from the legs, but after a short time you will experience discomfort as blood flow is constricted in the flesh between the seat bones (ischial tuberosities) and the flat plank. The weight of the upper body is concentrated on a small area of flesh immediately below these bones.

A comfortable wooden seat is achieved by spreading the body's weight over a larger area, so there are no points of intense pressure leading to restricted blood flow. With two seat bones in our bottoms, seats should ideally be hollowed down to two low points, and these will tend to be slightly closer to the spindle platform than to the front edge of the seat. The hollowing will then automatically be steeper at the back than the front, because the same depth will have to be achieved but over a shorter distance. The hollowing may have to be further exaggerated to prevent pressure on the coccyx (our vestigial tail). In any event the final surface should smoothly slope down to the low points in all directions.

How deep should the seat be hollowed? This is largely a matter of personal choice, but no more wood should remain than is necessary. In practice there is no need to leave more than ½in (1.3cm) of wood at the thinnest part of the seat (depth holes). If you do not wish to hollow as much, then consider using a thinner seat to begin with (the normal range is from 1¾ to 2in/3.5 to 5cm). Just remember that the seat is one of the heaviest parts of the chair, and it is usually appreciated if a chair is not too heavy to move about. Using the pillar drill, set the drill to your chosen depth by eye against the edge of the seat before drilling.

Position 1: excellent for softer wood and detailed work. Keep the forearms in contact with the thighs. All the work is done by the wrists and forearms.

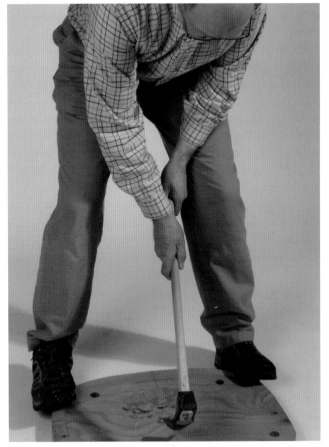

Position 2: ideal for rapid stock removal. Keep the left hand tight against the inner thigh, and pivot the tool about this point. This is a more upright stance.

SHAPING THE SEAT

As with all other operations in Windsor chairmaking, use a coarse tool for as long as possible before changing to a finer one.

The following sections will guide you through the processes for shaping a seat, but during the shaping it is vital that you keep the centre line on the back platform, and keep a trace of it at the front of the seat. It is essential to know where the centre line of the seat is when finding the centre of bows, arms and crests.

HOLLOWING

The bulk of the hollowing is achieved with an adze, and wood will continue to be removed until the bottoms of the depth holes are exposed.

Two alternative stances can be taken while adzing, and if you have a weak back, then the job can be done while sitting on a stool. In order to adze wood safely it is crucial that you have control over the blade. The blade needs to remove wood just where you intend (otherwise you can ruin the seat), and it must never be allowed to hit your foot or ankle.

Control of the tool comes from limiting the movement of the blade to the intended direction, and this is achieved by bracing against your body. My preferred stance is to hold the seat with the edges of the feet, and while bending the knees considerably, rest my forearms on the tops of my thighs. This stance immediately restricts the possible movement of the hands and has the added benefit of relieving the strain on the back.

Grasp the handle of the adze in your two hands (hands together and fairly low on the handle) and then swing the tool using only the wrists. You will find that if you maintain this position you will be unable to damage your feet or ankles. Make sure that your forearms remain in tight contact with your thighs.

Adjust the angle of the blade by moving your feet backwards and forwards, and by moving the hands up and down the handle. The blade should enter the wood and then exit leaving a clean, scalloped cut. It may take several swings to complete the cut, but the finished result should be smooth.

Do not rush the swing. The tool is heavy and will sap your strength rapidly if you attempt to move it much faster than gravity allows. Think of a pendulum and try to imitate the rhythm, assisting gravity rather than working against it. Golfers will recognize the similarity to their swing.

Start adjacent to the depth holes and work outwards, and it may be worth drawing concentric lines around the holes as a guide. The blade will cut better in the direction of the grain,

The travisher can remove wood quickly and accurately from the seat after adzing.

but it is important to work from all angles to produce a smooth profile. Work out from the holes a few inches in one direction, and then turn the seat through 180 degrees and repeat. This should produce a roughly oval hollow. Continue this process outwards (perhaps half way to the edge), and then return to the centre and remove more wood.

Do not try to adjust the shape of the resulting slope with the adze beyond creating a slope down towards the holes. Detailed shaping will be done quickly and in a controlled way with the travisher. Continue with the adze until the bottoms of the holes are exposed (not removed altogether) and the cut surface is within approximately ¼in (6mm) of the back platform and 1in (2.5cm) of the front.

At this point change to the travisher. Running it on the nose in front of the blade, move it steadily back and forth in a pendulum motion. Always cut with the tool moving away from the body so that the thumbs can push it directly behind the blade. This tool works best against the grain.

Smooth off the surface from the adze, extend the cut edge back to the lines that you have marked, and excavate to the bottom of the depth holes. Then create smooth curves between the top edge and where the depth holes were.

MAKING SPACE FOR THE THIGHS

Whatever the style of the seat, wood will need to be removed from the front to smooth the surface under the thighs. Most seat blanks when viewed from the front will need to have a 'w' shape of some form marked on the front edge, this line representing the depth to which the top surface is excavated; however, the exact treatment will depend on whether it is an English or American chair.

English: Remove wood from the front edge at approximately 45 degrees between the high point on the side edge and the centre point, on each side. The shaping is then completed by rounding over the resulting ridge so that there is a smooth rise and fall from the front edge into the main hollowed part of the seat.

American: In both shield and oval seats, remove all the wood (leaving a mildly convex surface) between the 'w' line, the ends of the spindle platform and the edge of the previously hollowed area. Once this is done, a sharp ridge will remain that must be rounded over with a rasp or spokeshave. The low point on a shield seat will be roughly over the front leg tenon, while on an oval seat it will be half way between the pommel (where the centre line crosses the front edge of the seat) and the spindle platform.

Spokeshaves and rasps are the tools of choice for these jobs. On softwood spokeshaves will be quicker at forming the 'cheeks', but a very aggressive rasp may be easier in hardwood. Rasps are ideally suited for rounding over, and much of the surface can be cleaned up with a finely set spokeshave.

On an American chair ensure that the ends of the spindle

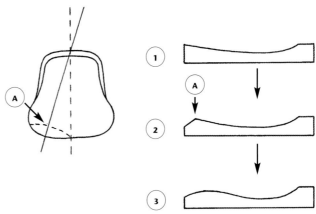

Using a rasp to create a convex surface. Work with a pendulum motion opposite to the curve to be created.

Removing wood to shape the seat.

Convex surfaces can be created with spokeshaves as well as rasps.

platform are crisply defined, and continue the slope from the hollow section around to the edge. A gouge may be used to define this edge, followed by spokeshave or rasp.

BOTTOM EDGE OF THE SEAT

With pine it may be possible to chamfer and round-over the lower edge of the seat with a drawknife, but this is not a realistic option with woods such as elm.

The chamfer around the bottom edge of an English chair (½ to ¾in/13 to 19mm wide) should be made at approximately 45 degrees. A spokeshave is probably the best tool to do this with. A vertical section then remains between the top of the chamfer and the spindle platform, and the hollowed section at the front: this surface will be covered in vertical bandsaw marks. A drum sander with, say, 40-grit paper will make short work of removing these saw marks, and the resulting sanding marks can be quickly removed with a scraper.

On American chairs the chamfer around the front of the seat can be slightly rounded, but should be close to 45 degrees. The purpose of this is to reduce the visible thickness of the seat everywhere so that the edge of the seat has no structural purpose other than to support the thighs of the sitter.

The back edge below the spindle platform needs to look more substantial, and sufficiently strong to support the elements of the back of the chair. This area can be shaped with drawknife and spokeshaves.

A quarter-round on the bottom edge, whilst keeping the remainder vertical, leaves a visually vague bottom edge. In my opinion it is better to create a curve that never drops more than 60 degrees from the vertical, and which then tapers to the top surface. The resulting edge is chamfered at 45 degrees.

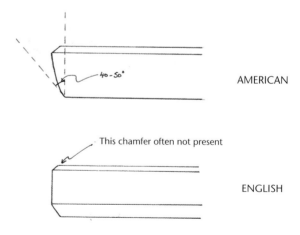

Some profiles are more attractive than others. A tapering curve is more attractive than a quarter-round with a vertical face.

SMOOTHING THE SURFACE

Once all the shaping has been done, the surface will still need to be cleaned up. Careful use of the travisher and spokeshaves will create surfaces that need very little further work, though frequently small areas of difficult grain will have torn somewhere and will need to be removed.

Abrasives are not the answer at this stage. A sharp cabinet scraper is much coarser and will remove blemishes rapidly. Use the scraper (curved or straight) only along the grain, and do not feel that you must remove all the ripples from seat hollowing. The final surface must be smooth to the touch, but not necessarily flat. A surface that is similar to beaten copper is beautiful and shows clearly that it has been created by hand, though this may be easier to create in a hardwood such as elm, than in a softer wood.

Any roughness remaining after using the scraper will be removed rapidly with abrasives. I would never expect to spend much more than ten minutes sanding a seat; any more means that you have not prepared it well enough previously.

Size the tenon with a spanner acting as callipers.

Making a Stool

The following sections describe how to assemble the undercarriage for a stool or chair.

Adding the Legs

Once the legs are dry they can be fitted into the seat. In fact although it is important that the tenons of legs and stretchers are dry, it is preferable that the swells (where the centre stretchers fit into the side stretchers) should retain some moisture, as the continued shrinkage of this wood helps to lock the stretcher tenons in place. Thus it is better to make and use legs within a short time, rather than making batches and allowing them to dry uniformly. If making legs well in advance, do not dry them fully (perhaps keep them outside), and then complete the drying just prior to use.

Return the legs to the lathe, sand them with one pass of 240 grit (if they were wet-sanded), and size the tenon to fit the seat mortices. A spanner is an ideal calliper for this operation as it cannot change its size. However, do not assume that it will always make perfect-sized tenons – try it first on scrap wood. Different makes of drill make slightly different sized holes even though they are nominally the same size. Do not be afraid to increase the width of the spanner with a file if it tends to make loose tenons. If the tenon is slightly too tight, carefully adjust it by sanding until it fits snugly, but not so tight that it cannot readily be rotated and removed.

Once all the legs are fully inserted into the seat, rotate them until the bull's eyes of the front and back legs face each other. This orientation is chosen so that the maximum possible shrinkage of the leg will occur around the stretcher tenons.

When the legs are correctly aligned, make an index mark on each leg and the seat, and number them, so that each leg can be removed from the seat and be replaced exactly as planned. At the same time mark around the top of each tenon at the top surface of the seat, and mark on the position for a saw kerf to accept a wedge when finally glueing up. This kerf must run perpendicular to the grain of the seat, otherwise it will split.

Remove the legs from the seat; using a bandsaw, cut off the excess wood from the top of each tenon, and make the slot for the wedge. Return the legs to the seat.

The legs are now ready to be drilled to accept the side stretchers. American legs almost always have a scribed line that marks the height of the stretchers from the seat. If you do

Number the leg and the seat, and make an index mark
for orientation.

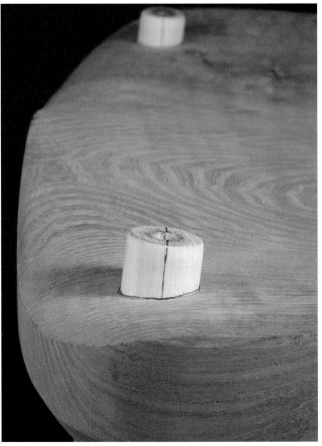

The kerfs for the wedges must be aligned across the grain
of the seat.

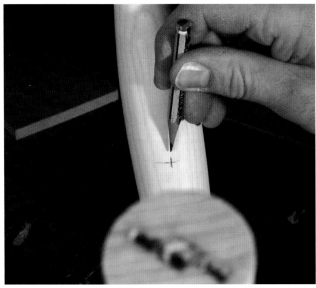

Look over the top of the opposite leg to mark the point for
drilling the stretcher mortice.

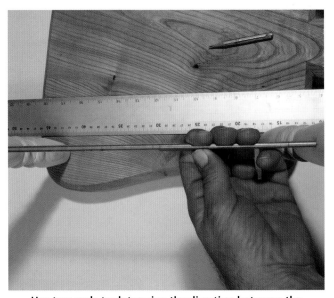

Use two rods to determine the direction between the
stretcher mortices.

not have this feature then mark points on each leg an equal distance up (along the legs) from the seat. This gives the height at which to drill, but a second mark must be made to ensure that the drill makes a hole in the centre of the leg. Look over the top of the opposite leg with one eye, and eyeball the centre of the leg at the height mark (or scribed line). This is the point to drill, which will give equal amounts of wood on each side of the hole.

Many chairmakers will then measure the angle between the leg and stretcher, remove the leg, and drill it while holding it in a vice or other jig. However, a simpler, quicker and more accurate method is to drill the legs in situ, without measuring any angles. A short drill and bit are ideal for this job. The tip of the drill is placed on one mark, while the back of the drill (you will need a centre mark) is aligned with the mark on the opposite leg. This gives the correct alignment for drilling.

Unfortunately you may not possess a drill that is sufficiently short to fit between the two legs, and a modification to the process will be needed.

Provided the front and back legs are in the same plane, remove one of the pair of legs and place a ruler along the edges of the seat mortices. This will give the direction in which to drill. Then place the tip of the drill bit on the mark and line the drill up parallel to the ruler. To obtain the correct orienta-tion 'up and down' it is useful to have another pair of eyes looking from the side. Have the second person hold a ruler against the two legs on the other side of the chair, lining it up with the two drilling marks that have been made previously. They can then advise 'up or down' to align the drill correctly.

If you have to do this on your own, wind the auger screw into the leg to hold it in position (lined up with the ruler) and, holding it in this position, glance from the side of the drill to check whether it is lined up with the marks on the other pair of legs. A little practice will allow you to do this with ease, and in any event there is considerable flexibility in the system, which will cope with small errors.

If your legs are not in the same plane, then line up the drill (or a pair of rods) between the two marks, and set the ruler parallel to this direction. Make a line on the seat against the ruler so that it can be reset for each leg without further effort. Then drill as before.

When drilling legs you should aim for deep mortices, but without the drill emerging from the other side of the leg; 7/8in (22mm) depth usually works well for the side stretchers in the leg, while ¾in (19mm) should be sufficient in the smaller-diameter side stretchers for the centre stretcher.

Depending on the type of drill, either insulating tape or a line scored with a hacksaw can act as a depth indicator. Take care with tape as it will tend to move up the drill if it comes into contact with the leg.

Fitting Stretchers

Each leg should now have a mortice drilled ready for the side stretchers. The stretchers have been made from an over-long blank so they can be made to fit the individual chair. Even when the same chair is made repeatedly, the length of stretch-ers will vary. Slight looseness of the leg in the seat will translate into a significant difference in stretcher length, and the holes are unlikely to be identical in depth.

Measure the distance between the bottoms of the opposing holes using two sticks held together (4mm dowelling works well). Make a mark on the sticks, remove them from the legs and realign the mark. Measure the length and add ¼in (6mm). This additional length will cause the stretchers to push the legs apart and create tension and compression in the undercar-riage when it is assembled. The stretchers will stretch the legs

Align the drill with the ruler (from above). Align with the drilling marks on the other pair of legs (from the side).

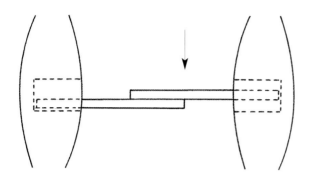

Use two dowels or rods to measure from the bottom of one mortice to the bottom of the other. Make a mark on one stick, remove and reassemble at the mark and measure. Add ¼" for 'stretch'.

apart, and eventually if the glue in the joint fails this extra length will also prevent the mechanical joint from failing.

FORMING TENONS

American stretchers will have a scribed line to mark their centre. If your English stretcher doesn't have this feature, then mark the centre with a pencil. Halve the calculated overall length and mark this distance on either side of the centre line. These marks represent the ends of the completed stretcher.

Measure back from the ends by the chosen length of the tenons – say, ⅞in/22mm for a side stretcher – and make another mark. Spin the stretcher up on the lathe and you should be able to see the position of each tenon (between the two marks at each end).

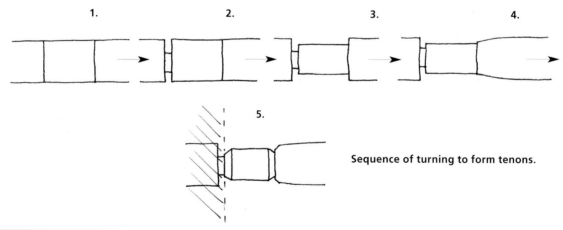

1.   2.   3.   4.

5.

Sequence of turning to form tenons.

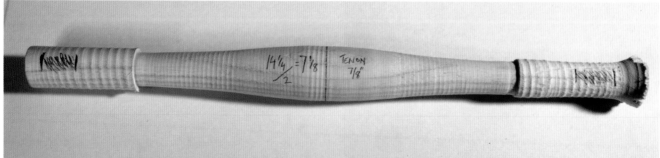

A stretcher marked up for tenoning: the length between the bottom of the mortices is 14in (35cm); add ¼in for 'stretch': 14¼in divided by 2 = 7⅛in on either side of the centre line; the tenon is ⅞in long.

Sizing the tenon with a spanner.

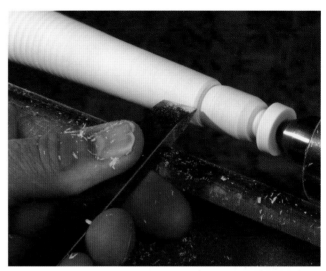

The completed tenon.

The tenons are made slightly over-size and are driven into the mortice, making a one-shot joint. There is no opportunity to dry-fit the stretchers first, but provided you have not made any errors of measurement it works well and is quick. Experiment with your drill and a spanner of the same nominal size, and expect to have to widen the throat of your spanner to make an oversize tenon. Trial and error on scrap wood is recommended before working on your chair legs.

Use the following routine to make the tenons:

- Using a parting tool, make a groove tight up to the end of the tenon, but on the outside so that the diameter is less than the final tenon size. The end of the tenon is now physically delineated.
- Size the tenon (between the two marks) with the spanner in the usual way.
- Blend the stretcher into the tenon, leaving a small shoulder.
- Take a skew chisel and, holding it perpendicular to the stretcher, bevel the end of the tenon; flip it over and form a reverse bevel at the other end of the tenon; and finally create a small bevel on the shoulder.
- Repeat at the other end of the stretcher.
- Sand the stretchers (not the tenons) before removing them from the lathe and cutting off the excess.

FITTING THE SIDE STRETCHERS

The tenons have been made over-size, and so if they are driven into the mortice without any further adjustment they will tend to split the leg. Any split will run along the length of the leg, rather than across it, as the wood is much stronger in this direction. To prevent splitting, take the stretchers and pare a small amount of wood from the 'bull's eye' sides of each tenon. A broad gouge is ideal for this job, and it is made easier by the reverse bevel.

Glue can be put into the leg mortice using a small stick; then lay the leg on the bench and place the tenon over the mortice. Make sure that the flats (the bull's eye surfaces of the tenon) are on each side of the leg, then hold it at the approximate

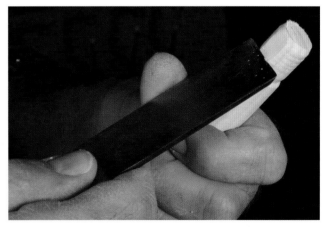

Remove wood from each side of the stretcher tenon so that it doesn't split the leg when driven into the tight hole.

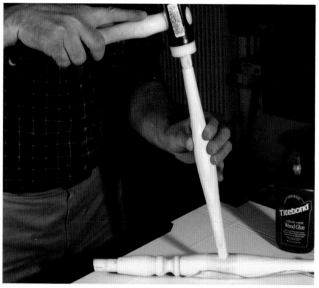

Tap the stretcher into the leg with the tenon's 'flats' on either side of the leg.

Stretcher-leg joint. Note how the two parts have blended together to hide all sign of the tenon.

angle of the hole, and drive it home with a mallet. The shoulder should be pushed tight up to the leg, hiding both it and the tenon.

Put glue into the mortice of the other leg, then line up the two legs and pound the tenon home. Repeat for the other pair of legs, and insert the legs into the seat.

FITTING THE CENTRE STRETCHER

Repeat the whole routine for the centre stretcher, but ensure that the holes are drilled straight across the seat rather than perpendicular to the stretcher.

Final Assembly of the Undercarriage

The four legs and three stretchers should now form a complete unit. Don't worry if the leg tenons do not precisely line up with the hole in the seat, as the whole unit will adjust as it is pounded home.

Put glue in each of the seat holes and knock in the legs until they are tight up to the seat. Then turn it over and drive wedges, with glue, into the saw cuts until they sound tight. Note that even if the wedges are aligned across the grain of the seat, if they are hit too hard there is a risk of a split devel-

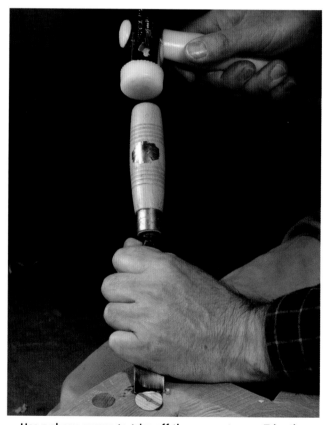

Use a sharp gouge to trim off the excess tenon. Trim the wedge off first.

oping, particularly with a soft seat material such as pine or tulip wood.

Leave the glue to dry, then trim off the wedges and excess tenon with a saw followed by mallet and gouge. To produce a finish flush with the surface complete the process with a scraper and then abrasives.

Levelling Up

The stool that you have now assembled is unlikely to be stable since the leg blanks do not need to be carefully cut to identical lengths and the angle of each leg may be slightly (though hopefully not visibly) different. Now the seat must be put into the correct orientation relative to the floor, and the legs must be cut to a correct length to hold the seat at the ideal height.

The seat of a good chair should tilt backwards slightly to prevent the sitter's bottom sliding out from underneath him. The backwards tilt and the hollowing of the seat both play a part in this; an additional benefit is that more of the sitter's weight is transferred to the back of the chair, thus further reducing the weight on the bottom.

You will need the following equipment to level a stool:

*   Three wedges
*   Spirit level
*   24in (60cm) ruler
*   Pencil with holder (see photo)
*   ½in (13mm) thick block

Find a flat and level piece of floor (this may be difficult), or set up a work surface that is truly horizontal. Place the stool on this surface with the spirit level across the back of the chair. Use wedges to centre the bubble and make sure there is no wobble by filling any resulting gaps with a wedge.

Place the ½in block on the back platform and lay the spirit level along the centre line resting on the block at the back. Holding either the two back or front legs flat on the ground,

First level the seat side to side with wedges.

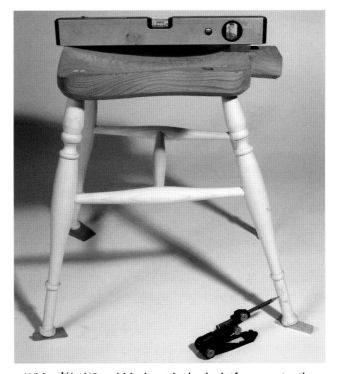

With a ½in (13mm) block on the back platform, centre the bubble of the level by raising/lowering the front/back. Finally draw around each leg at the required height above the floor to give the correct height of the seat once the legs have been cut off at the pencil marks.

Lay a straight edge along the centre line. Place a square on the back platform, perpendicular to the centre line, and look over the back of the arm. The centre point can be marked when the edge of the square lines up with the centre line.

Drilling through an arm, aiming at a point on the seat.

raise the opposite pair of legs (using the wedges) until the bubble is centred, and stabilize the stool. The seat is now correctly orientated relative to the floor, but is (hopefully!) too high.

Measure the height of the nose of the seat above the floor, and calculate the amount to be cut off each leg. The conventional height of most Windsor chairs today is 18in (45cm). Once the amount of cut-off has been calculated, adjust the pencil holder, or build up blocks so that the tip of the pencil is the desired height over the ground. Then carefully run the pencil around the bottom of each leg and cut off the excess: this will produce angled cuts that will leave the bottom of the legs flat on the floor.

Finally, rasp a bevel around the bottom of each leg to prevent it from chipping if used on a hard floor.

Making the Superstructure

Many of the techniques involved in assembling the superstructure of a Windsor chair, whatever the style (side chair, armchair), are the same. However, armchairs will require more techniques simply because of the addition of arms and armposts.

Finding the Centre

Virtually all chairs are bilaterally symmetrical (because humans are) and at some stage in making the superstructure it becomes necessary to find the central axis of symmetry (the centre line) so that the spindles can be arranged evenly on either side of it. Most chairs have an uneven number of spindles so the central spindle lies on the axis of symmetry – although it can be argued that having a gap in the centre – having an even number of spindles – is more favourable to the sitter's back as there will not be a spindle directly behind the spine. In fact in practice it makes little difference to the comfort of a chair, as we often sit on a chair slightly off centre, thereby nullifying any benefits of a central gap. My preference is for a central spindle, which visually defines the central axis.

To find the centre of a bow, arm or crest, hold them in place and lay a long ruler along the centre line of the seat. Then place a square on the back platform, perpendicular to, and touching the edge of the ruler. Look over the top of the bow so that you can see the vertical edge of the square and the horizontal edge of the ruler. Move your head until these edges coincide, and make a mark where those edges appear to cross the bow.

Repeat the process with the ruler and square on opposite sides of the seat's centre line, and remark the bow. If the marks do not coincide, then split the difference: the variation will come from the seat not being perfectly flat. Even if the seat blank were flat initially, the process of removing so much wood during the shaping often causes it to curl up slightly.

Drilling Through one Piece of Wood while Aiming at Another

The spindles of many chairs pass through arms and bows (bow-back, double bow), and these holes need to line up with the mortices in the seat. If you try this you will find that it is impossible to see the mark that you are aiming for while drilling, and so a systematic approach is needed to achieve the correct direction.

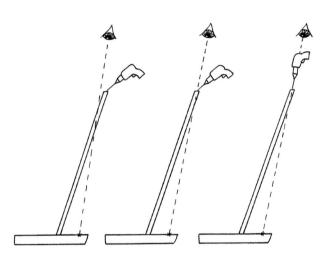

Drilling through a bow aiming at a mark on the seat: With one eye look over the front of the bow at the mark on the seat; move your head back until the mark on the seat is directly under the centre of the bow; raise the drill until the centre of the back covers the tip of the drill.

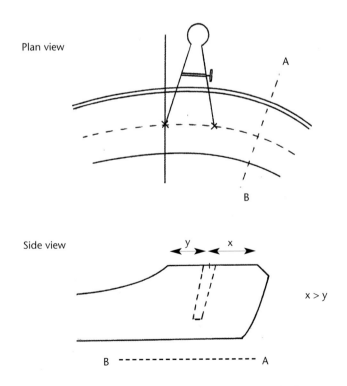

Leave plenty of wood around the spindle mortices in the seat particularly if the seat wood is soft and liable to split.

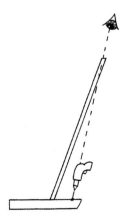

Drilling a hole in the seat aiming through a hole in an arm: place tip of drill on the mark; with one eye centre the tip of the drill in the hole; bring the drill up until the centre mark is centred in the hole.

Place the tip of the drill on the point in the bow where the hole is to be made. Drop the drill back and look over the front of the bow so that you can just see the spot on the seat that you will be aiming at.

Move your head backwards until the spot on the seat has moved so that it is directly underneath the tip of your drill (judgement will be required). Now your eye, the tip of the drill and the spot on the seat are all in line.

Fix the position of the drill tip in your mind's eye, and then raise the drill so that the mark on its back (the centre point) covers the tip of the drill. The drill is now lined up: drill the hole.

This procedure will require practice before confidence develops, so practise first on scrap wood before drilling the holes in your seat. Provided you understand the principle behind the system, and have faith in it, then with practice every hole will be correct.

You may need to create your own mark on the back of the drill. To do this, place a long bit in the chuck; then take a straight edge and hold it parallel to the bit along the side of the drill, and use this to mark the point on the back immediately behind the drill bit.

Drilling Crests

The approach will be different depending on whether the crest is to be supported on rigid back-posts, or solely on flexible spindles. If the chair has back-posts then it must be mounted on these before fitting the spindles, but if there are only spindles then it should be mounted on the central spindle first, and then fitted on to the others.

A SPINDLE-ONLY CHAIR
On the underside of the crest mark the centre point (you will probably have a centre mark from when it was bent) and hold it on the bench, making adjustments with wedges so that the two faces are vertical (or at least in the correct orientation to a vertical spindle, if the crest has a tapered cross-section).

Set up two squares in front of the crest: one should be parallel to the crest, and the other perpendicular. Align the drill with the two squares so that it is vertical, and drill to the required depth (say, ¾in/ 19mm).

Mark on the positions of the other spindles along the centre line of the crest. In most chairs the spindles are equidistant. Then, holding the crest on the bench, with each end touching the edge of the bench, draw lines through the spindle marks perpendicular to the bench, and make marks on the front of the crest where the lines cross the edge.

Fit the crest on to the centre spindle. Then holding a rod against the appropriate mark on the front face of the crest with the other end on the spindle mark on the seat, draw lines on each side of the rod on the face of the crest. These lines will give the direction in which their mortices should be drilled.

Set the crest up on the bench as before. Place a drill bit in the first hole as an additional check that you will be drilling into the centre of the crest. Set up a square perpendicular to the crest against which you can judge 'front and back' movement of the drill, and then align it 'left and right' with the lines drawn either side of the rod on the front face of the crest. Check that everything is aligned, and drill.

Repeat this process for each rod and finally mount the crest, checking and adjusting so that it is at an equal height above

Drilling a crest with the direction marked on to the front of the crest (left-to-right), and a square to help align the drill front-to-back.

the seat on each side, and so that there is sufficient spindle tenon in each hole.

A CHAIR WITH BACK-POSTS

Hold the crest against the tenons of the back-posts, ensuring that the centre of the crest is centred between the back-posts. Lightly mark the crest on either side of the tenon on each side. Draw a final bold line between the two previous lines to give the position and direction of the tenons.

Hold the crest upside down against the edge of the bench, and draw lines perpendicular to the bench from the bold line on the front surface to the back surface. The mid-point of this line is where the hole should be drilled, using the bold lines for direction.

Mount the crest on the back-posts, and check that it is at the same height on both sides. Mark out the spindle positions between the back-posts, and using a long dowel held against the point on the seat and marks on the crest, draw on the direction lines for each tenon. Drill each hole as previously described.

DRILLING SPINDLE MORTICES IN THE SEAT

Method 1 (aiming): If ever there was a candidate for drilling by aiming, this is it. Sharp auger drill bits can be started at the correct angle without the need to start vertically, and then adjusted to the desired angle, leaving an over-sized hole. This will cause little, if any, tear-out of the seat.

Place the tip of the drill on the mark on the seat. Look though the hole in the arm/bow, and centre the tip of the drill in the hole. Then centre the mark on the back of the drill in the hole, and drill.

Method 2 (aiming): English chairs do not have 'through' holes in their bows and arms, but the holes in the seat must still line up accurately with the corresponding holes in the bow. There are two alternative methods that will be described.

The first system requires judgment, but is quick and accurate with practice. The greatest benefit is that no angles need be known, and therefore there is minimal set-up and a reduced chance of making errors in the set-up. You will need to mark out the positions of the spindles on the arm/bow before drilling, as these marks will be used to align the drill. The procedure is as follows:

- Place the tip of the drill on the mark on the seat, and tilt the drill back away from the arm/bow.
- Look over the front of the arm/bow so that the tip of the drill is just visible.
- Move your head back so that the tip of the drill moves under the arm/bow to a position under the centre of the mark on the arm/bow. Your eye, the centre of the arm/bow, and the tip of the drill are now aligned.
- Raise the drill so that the mark on the back of the drill is directly under the mark on the arm/bow.
- Your drill is now aligned, so drill.

Method 3 (sight lines): This method requires the sight lines and angles of the spindles in the seat to be determined so that the holes can be drilled using the tilting table on the drill press. If you do not have an existing chair to work from, then hold two pieces of thin dowel together so that one end of each is in contact with the marks on the seat and the arm/bow.

Make sure that the seat is held horizontally (not on its trimmed legs and tilting backwards); then holding the dowels in place, move around them until they appear to be perpendicular to the seat. At this point your direction of sight is the sight line of the spindle. Mark it on the seat (and make a note of it for future reference).

The angle can be measured using a simple protractor, or even a digital angle finder. Make sure to measure in the direction of the sight line.

With a sight line and angle for the spindle the hole can be drilled on a tilting table or with a hand drill and a bevel guage.

Drilling Blind Mortices in Bows and Arms

If the arm is held parallel to the seat (as in most English chairs) then the sight lines and angles will be the same for both the seat and the arm. Determine these using the technique described above, and drill the blind holes in the arm using a drill press.

Drilling a bow poses a different challenge, as the sight lines and angles for the mortices in the seat do not transfer easily to a curved bow. Instead, mark the positions for the mortices on the bow. Place the bottom of a long dowel (or threaded rod) in the seat mortice, and line it up with the mark on the bow.

Use a pencil to mark the front of the bow on both sides of the dowel – this is the direction of lean. While doing this take note of the angle between the dowel and the plane of the bow.

Hold the bow upside down in the vice. Use a screw auger to start the hole, and line it up with the marks on the front of the bow. Then maintaining the same direction, lean the drill back from the plane of the bow to give the correct angle, and begin to drill. Once a circular flat has been made, change to a forstner bit and drill to depth.

While it is difficult to achieve perfect alignment, the natural flexibility of wood will cope with small errors, and maximize your chances of a satisfactory joint.

Most of the techniques used in assembling side chair super-structures have now been covered, but a description of the steps (and any not yet covered) will now be given for several different styles of chair.

Lean the drill back from the plane of the bow.

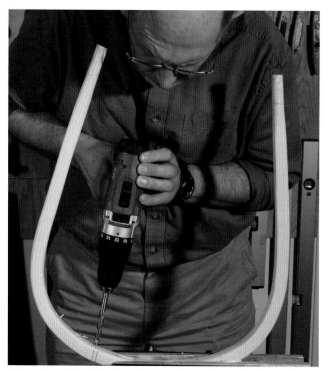

Align the drill with direction marks made on the front of the bow.

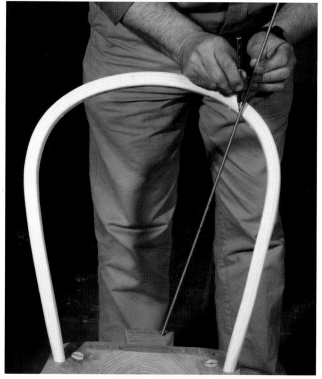

Using a rod to mark the bow with the direction line of the bracing spindle.

Bow-back Chair Superstructure

Tenons must be made at either end of the bow. The blank should have been slightly over-length so that crushed and distorted wood at each end can be cut off, leaving sound wood for the tenons.

Take the distance from the seat surface to the top of the bow, in the plane of the bow, and make a mark this distance from the edge of the bench. Draw a line perpendicular to the edge of the bench through the mark. Place the bow with the top edge on the mark, and make it symmetrical about the line on the bench. The edge of the bench represents seat level, so mark the bow 2in (5cm) beyond the bench and cut off the excess. This should give a slightly over-length tenon that can eventually be trimmed to size.

Use a plastic gauge to mark a circle of the correct diameter on the base of the tenon, and hold the arm of the bow vertically in the vice so that the tenon can be made comfortably with spokeshaves.

Spokeshave down to the circle, and then carefully form the tenon in the usual way, taking care to remove wood evenly from all round it, and keeping it snug on the gauge. If this tenon is too small it will never make a satisfactory joint in the

seat. Aim to make both tenons 1¾ in (4.5cm) long, and then test fit them in the seat. Check the height above the seat, and make the tenons longer if necessary. Continue until the bow sits in the ideal position, marking the fronts of the tenons at seat level with a pencil.

Cut off any excess tenon on the underneath of the seat, cutting parallel to the seat and leaving ⅛in (3mm) of tenon proud of the seat. This stub allows the end of the bow to spread slightly with a wedge so that it can never pull back through the hole even if the glue joint fails in due course. Mark the centre of the bow.

Mark the spindle positions on the spindle platform. Draw a line, using your fingers as a gauge, slightly closer to the centre of the seat than half way between the edge of the hollow and the edge of the outside chamfer. This maximizes the amount of seat wood around the tenons while being visually acceptable.

Mark on the positions of the spindles on the bow.

Drill the bow, using through holes for American chairs, and blind holes for English ones.

Drill the holes in the seat, lining up the drill with the holes in the bow.

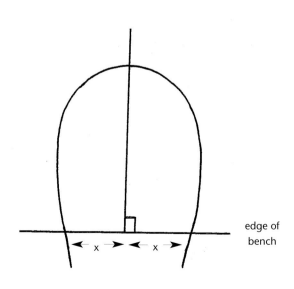

Lay the bow on the bench so that the edge intersects with the bow at 'seat level'. Measure 2" beyond the edge and cut off the excess.

Tenon on the end of a bow formed carefully with a small spokeshave and plastic gauge.

Test-fitting the bow.

Mark the edge of the bow on to the spindles, add sufficient length for the tenon, and cut off the excess.

Place glue in the holes, selecting the best long spindle for the centre position, and carefully drive in the spindles, watching the seat adjacent to the holes for any sign of splitting.

American chairs: Dry-fit the bow over the spindles inserting the bow tenons into the seat. Tap the bow into place with a soft mallet, and make any adjustments to the spindle tenons to allow the bow to enter the seat up to the pencil marks previously made.

Trim off excess tenon protruding from the bow, leaving a ⅛ in (3mm) stub.

English chairs: Fit the bow with the spindles in front of the bow. Move each spindle to its position on the bow, and mark where it crosses the bow. Cut off excess spindle, leaving the correct length for the tenon and using a broad gouge form tenons on the ends of the spindles. Use a plastic gauge to test the tenons, which can be made faceted and slightly over-size, as on the base.

Place glue in the mortices (bow and seat), and assemble the back. The English bow will need to be knocked into place,

seating the spindle tenons in their mortices, while the American chair should slide together quite easily.

Tap in a glued wedge into the ends of the bow tenons.

American chair only: Split the ends of the tenons with a chisel across the grain of the bow, and tap in glued wedges until tight. Leave until the glue is dry, and then trim off with a saw, followed by a gouge. Finally clean up with a scraper and abrasives.

Fanback Chair Superstructure

Insert the back-posts into the seat, having formed tenons at both ends. Trim the tenon under the seat, and glue and wedge it in place (as for the bow). If using ribbon slats in an English comb-back, insert a dowel through the side of the seat and the slat itself.

Drill and fit the crest.

Drill spindle holes in the seat, lining up the drill with the holes in the crest. Glue and tap in the spindles.

Mount the crest on the back-posts, and mark the level of the bottom of the crest on each spindle while it is held in the correct position. Trim each spindle to leave the tenon the correct length. Cut the spindle tenons slightly shorter than the depth of the mortices so they do not bottom out during assembly.

Place glue in all the crest holes, and tap on the crest. In some cases it may be necessary to hold the crest down on the spindles with a sash cramp positioned between the crest and the seat.

Drill holes through the front face of the crest through the two outside tenons (back-posts) and centre spindle, stopping just before the drill emerges through the back face. Make small wooden pegs approximately 3.5mm in diameter (called treenails), insert glue into the holes, and tap the pegs home. Trim and clean up. The three pegs will hold the crest on the spindles long after the glue may have failed. Depending on the arrangement of the spindles and the shape of the crest, some joints in the crest may be in tension and others in compression as the sitter leans back. These pegs are essential, and attractive at the same time.

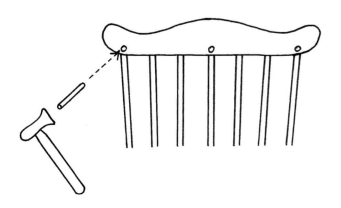

A crest should be pinned in three places.

Arm-chair Superstructure

The main challenge in assembling the superstructure of an armchair lies in the fact that the arm is not socketed into the seat, but is attached to spindles and arm-posts some height above the seat. This requires an arrangement to hold it in the correct position so that all the parts can be correctly aligned.

However, before any holes can be drilled it may be necessary to make the hands (the ends of the arms) larger so they can accept tenons from the arm-posts; they also look better. Blocks of wood may need to be glued on to the arms. This is standard practice on American chairs, but is less usual in English chairs. The early English chairs often had arms made from a yew stem, which was bent in the round and then shaped appropriately. The excess width allowed for hands to be formed without having to glue on additional pieces. If you study these chairs you will often find the sapwood on the outside of the hand, showing that the maximum width of the stem was used.

It is also quite possible to leave a bow to be bent wider at the ends, so that there is sufficient wood to shape the hand when bent. A bending strap will still support most of the wood when bending.

GLUING ON HANDS
For a successful glue joint, both the end of the arm and the block of wood must be jointed. Contact needs to be achieved over the length of the joint as it will be subjected to considerable stress each time the sitter pushes himself out of the chair. In addition, the tenon of the arm-post may cross the joint, adding to the possible stresses. The butt joint is not reinforced with dowels, but will rely on glue and the quality of preparation for strength. 250-year-old joints are still sound, so it works!

Instead of holding the arm in the vice and balancing the plane on the narrow edge, reverse the normal procedure and clamp the plane in the vice and move the arm over the blade, more like using an electric jointer. Gloves are highly recommended as the plane blade is exposed and will flatten your hand given a chance!

Make sure that the plane blade is sharp and square and set fine. Hold the arm vertically above the plane (even if the surface to be planed is not parallel to the plane, having twisted during bending) and make cuts until the arm sits in the correct orientation. Then press down with both hands directly over the length to be jointed, and make enough passes to flatten

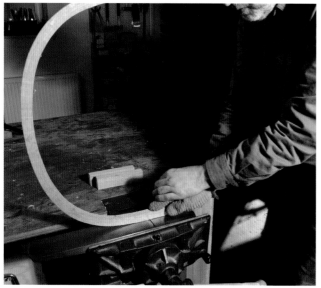

Holding the plane in the vice, joint the sides of the arm and blocks.

Glue the jointed blocks on to the arm.

the whole surface.

Repeat this with the block to be added, and test the two surfaces together. No gaps should be visible.

Hold the arm in the vice with the flat surface uppermost. Apply glue to the block, and rub it on to the arm until the glue begins to grip. Then clamp and leave to cure.

It is helpful if the blocks are slightly thicker than the arm, and slightly longer than the final hand. This excess will make the shaping of the hand easier.

Superstructure for Chair with Turned Arm-Posts

HOLDING THE ARM IN POSITION

An arm can be held in the correct position by balancing it on just three points. It is useful to make up dummy arm-posts that are the same height as the underside of the hand. Cut them at roughly the correct angle so that the arm sits easily. These can be made of any scrap wood.

The third point should be in the position of the central spindle. In the same way as the arm-posts, make up a spindle in a

Balance the arm on three points to give the correct orientation above the seat.

block so that it sits at the same height as the bottom of the arm in this position. The block should span the seat and have a centre line that can be aligned with the centre line of the seat. It is also important to have an angled line on the side of the block that shows where the spindle touches the seat.

With these aids in place the arm can be rested on the three points, and you can begin marking up ready for drilling holes.

Position the arm carefully, evening up the overhang of the hands beyond the arm posts, and ensuring that the central spindle is just forward of the centre of the bow (the hole will be angled starting on the top surface closer to the back, and emerging underneath closer to the front edge of the arm).

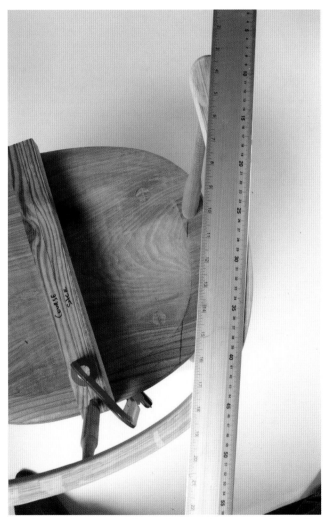

Look over the arm and draw a line on the arm parallel to the sight line on the seat.

Then carefully draw round the top of the arm post on the underside of the arm. This is where the holes will be drilled into the arm.

However, one needs both a position (just marked) and the angle/direction (sight line) for the hole. Keeping the arm in place on the three points, lay a long ruler over the arm and align it with the sight line on the top surface of the seat which was used to drill the holes for the arm-posts in the seat. Try to place the rule so that it passes roughly through the hand where the hole will be drilled – this does not have to be exact. Mark the line on the arm, both at the hand and at the back.

Remove the arm and produce the same line on the underside of the arm by running the line down each edge and joining up these marks (in the same way that you transferred the centre line of the seat to the other side after the seat had been cut out).

Prior to drilling the hands, the only other information required is the angle. If the arm is to be parallel to the seat, then drill at the same angle as the arm-post holes in the seat. If it is to be lower at the back than the front then increase the angle by, say, 2 degrees. Most early English chairs had the underside of their arms parallel to the seat, but sometimes had the top surfaces tilting down towards the front.

American chairs normally had their arms tilting back, and require a larger angle than the arm-post angle. There are some exceptions to this: Philadelphia chairs often had arm-posts tilted a couple of degrees from the vertical, but with arms perpendicular to the arm-post. In this situation the holes can be drilled with a pillar drill to achieve an accurate right-angle.

Assuming that the holes are to be drilled at an angle, clamp the arm on to a block of wood, with the underside facing up. Set a bevel gauge at the required angle and lay it parallel to the sight line. Place the point of the drill on the spot, and adjust the angle to match the bevel gauge, taking care to remain in the plane of the sight line. Then drill.

English chairs usually had straight tenons on the top of the arm-posts (turned arm-posts were virtually unheard of in the earlier Georgian chairs), while American chairs often used a tapered joint. The tapered tenon is easy to create on the lathe using a skew chisel flat on the rest, and the tapered mortice must be made in a separate step using a reamer (held at the correct angle in the same way as the drill).

When the mortices are made, test-fit the arm to the posts, and make any adjustments to depth and angle until the arm sits correctly.

(a) Drill the hand, leaning the drill in the plane of the sight-line and guided by the bevel gauge set at the appropriate angle.

b) Ream out the hole at the same angle

c) Completed joint.

Chair with curved arm supports (yet to be fitted). The bow has been mounted on eight short spindles prior to drilling for the long spindles and fitting the arm supports.

DRILLING FOR SPINDLES

Once the arm has been mounted on the arm-posts, the spindle holes can be drilled in the seat and arm.

Mark the spindle positions on the seat, beginning with the central spindle on the centre line and measuring outwards on each side. Check that the spacing between the final spindle and the arm-post is similar on each side; if it is not, then check the laying out. Otherwise adjust the spacing of the short spindles until they are even.

Find the centre point on the arm, and then mark on the spindle positions in the same way as for the seat.

Using the dummy central spindle to support the back of the arm, drill the holes in the arm, aiming at the marks on the seat.

Finally, using a right-angle drill under the arm, drill the mortices in the seat, lining up the drill with the holes in the arm.

Glue in the spindles and mount the arm on top, adjusting either spindles or holes to bring the arm to the correct height above the seat.

Superstructure for Chair with Steam-bent Arm Supports

Curved arm supports are not as structurally important as turned posts, because the joint between them and the arm is not as strong. A flat surface is created on the top of the arm support, which marries up with the underside of the arm, and is then pinned or, in later chairs, screwed together. The integrity of the superstructure is more dependent on the short spindles in these chairs than the arm supports. For this reason all the spindles can be fitted first, leaving the supports to be fitted and attached as a final step.

The curved arm supports should have tenons made on their bases long enough so that the top surface that marries with the arm can be brought up to the arm from below, with adjustments made until they fit together. The tenons will need to be accurate, otherwise gaps will be apparent at seat level.

The tops of the supports can be cut off on a bandsaw. If the sight lines for the supports in the seat lie straight across the seat (perpendicular to the centre line), then tilt the table to the same angle as the seat hole, and holding the tenon perpendicular to the blade against the mitre gauge, run the support through the blade at the correct height.

If the sight line is not at 90 degrees to the centre line, then adjust the mitre gauge by the same angle, and cut the tops as

before.

Do not cut tight to the line, but leave a small thickness for making adjustments to the cut surface with a block plane so that it fits tightly to the underside of the arm.

When fitted, secure with a cut nail or small screw. In either case a pilot hole passing through the support into the arm will ensure that the joint does not move when the screw or nail is inserted.

Fitting a Bow or Crest to an Armchair

A crest can be mounted in exactly the same way as was described for a side chair with a crest.

A bow mounted above the arm to make a double-bow or sack-back chair is tenoned through the arm, and has the long spindles fitted into or through it. The bow should be held in its correct orientation with each end on the arm at the insertion point, preferably with the spindles interlaced on either side of the bow, though this may not be possible if the spindles are too stiff.

The main challenge is to find the sight line for drilling the

Drilling the arm of a double-bow chair to accept the tenons of the top bow.

arm so that the tenon fits cleanly and the spindles intersect the top of the bow without too much bending.

With the tenons of the bow in position on the arm, look down the line of the tenon and project it by eye along the arm. Mark where this line crosses the edge of the arm to give a sight line when drilling.

Set a bevel gauge to the correct angle and attach it to the arm with a rubber band, lining it up with the sight line. Place the tip of the drill on the mark, and incline it in the plane of the sight line until it is at the same angle as the gauge, and drill.

Form tenons on the ends of the bow, and fit it to the arm. Then fit the spindles into the bow in exactly the same way as they are fitted in a bow-back chair. When glued up, wedge the bow tenons in the arm.

Adhesives

There is a wide range of glues available that can be used for chairmaking, but over the years I have settled on three. Many comparative tests have been conducted to find the 'best' glue, and while these give useful information, the final choice will depend on which products best suit your method of working.

PVA Glue

The glue that I do not use at all is white PVA glue. A bottle is probably to be found in most wood workshops, but the biggest problem is that it is water-based and causes parts to swell as soon as they come in contact with it. Take, for example, the joint between the legs and the seat, where the tenons should be snug, with no wobble, and the legs should be capable of being wound in and out without too much effort. However, when PVA glue is placed in the mortices and the leg tenon is inserted, the tenon will swell, causing it to lock in the mortice, usually before it can be pushed fully home. It is not uncommon for chairmakers to take club hammers to the legs to overcome this problem during assembly.

This abuse of the wood runs counter to the care that is taken at every other stage of chairmaking, and can be totally avoided

by choosing a different glue. However, if you can live with this drawback then it is an excellent adhesive.

Yellow Aliphatic Resin Glue

Sometimes it is necessary to make up seat blanks from several boards, if individual boards of sufficient width cannot be found. It is not sensible when gluing up a seat to reinforce it with biscuits or dowels, as these are likely to be exposed when the seat is excavated. However, the experience of makers over many years suggests that a plain butt joint is quite sufficient provided it is carefully made. The two surfaces should fit together without any discernible gaps along their length, and this may take considerable effort to achieve.

I make the joints for such seats with a planer, and it always surprises me that the way in which the board is pushed across the planer knives determines the success or failure of the process even when the machine is perfectly set up. I find that considerable downward pressure on the outfeed table is essential to get matching surfaces with no gaps at each end. If you

Aliphatic resin, hide and polyurethane glues all used in Windsor chairmaking.

use a mechanical planer you will have to develop a system that works for you as there is no room for compromise in this crucial joint.

My preferred glue for this type of joint is yellow aliphatic resin emulsion glue such as Titebond Original. The joint is stronger than the surrounding wood, and it is reassuring to test this occasionally by breaking an off-cut from a seat by hitting it against an edge along the glue line. Provided you made the joint well, it will be the wood that fails.

One of the most important characteristics of the glue to be used in the remainder for the chair is that it should be 'slippery' so that tight joints can be easily assembled, and in my experience two types of glue have these properties: polyurethane and hide (particularly liquid) glues.

Polyurethane and Liquid Hide Glues

Polyurethane glues are 'slippery' and have long open times – certainly long enough for assembling even the most complex Windsor chair, but excess glue foams up and this may be extruded from the joint if too much glue was initially added. This foam has no structural strength and can be easily picked off with a knife or sharp chisel, but the surface of any wood that it has been in contact with may need to be removed if the chair is eventually to be stained, as the glue will prevent absorption. This clean-up process can occur within about twenty minutes of making the joint if the environment is warm.

Liquid hide glue has the same lubricating property of polyurethane glue, but without the disadvantage of foaming. However, excess glue takes longer to 'go off', and so jobs such as cutting off the tops of spindles that protrude through bows will have to be delayed for longer than if polyurethane glue is used. Clean-up is easier as the glue is water-soluble, and a damp cloth is all that is necessary to remove excess. Buying hide glue in this form is relatively expensive, and the bottles have a shelf life that should not be exceeded, but the convenience is great. Unless you plan to make a large number of chairs the additional cost may be immaterial relative to the convenience.

The greatest benefit of using hide glue (of any type) is that it can be reversed with gentle heat and moisture. Hopefully as a chairmaker this will have no direct impact on your work, but in the future when a joint fails or a part breaks (as will inevitably happen at some point) the chair can be disassembled easily and the necessary repairs made. If a non-reversible glue such as polyurethane had been used, then the process will be much more difficult with a greater risk of damage during disassembly.

Finishing

Why do chairs have to be 'finished'? The first purpose of a finish is to protect the surface of the wood from becoming dirty. Chairs are generally made to be used, and wood is like a magnet for dirt. An 'unfinished' chair will quickly become grimy, particularly on the legs where it will be regularly kicked by the sitter or someone passing, and on the arm or bow where it may be handled by less-than-clean hands.

The second purpose of the finish is to enhance the look of the chair. It always surprises me that most non-furniture makers cannot see beyond the finish, or at least cannot imagine the piece with an alternative finish. For this reason the finish has to be good. However fine your chair, if the finish is poor, the general public will consider it a poor chair. This is not fair, but it is a fact.

Unfortunately making a chair is hard work, and the satisfaction of completing a chair is so great that the prospect of more work afterwards, particularly in a field that may not be familiar (finishing) is depressing. The result is that the minimum of effort tends to be expended in the hope that the chair will speak for itself. Sadly it is often the finish that speaks for itself, and the qualities of the chair are ignored.

Thus a good finish is essential if you wish someone to see the chair underneath it. If the finish is acceptable, then your chair will be looked at; if it is not, then however good the chair, it will be ignored. So it is worth a little effort to achieve a finish that people find acceptable, and one that doesn't take too much time and effort on top of the work that has already been done making the chair itself.

In spite of many excellent books written on the subject over the past twenty years, finishing remains as mysterious as alchemy to many. Finishing experts are loath to share their secrets for producing glowing surfaces that appear hundreds of years old, and this area will remain shrouded in mystery as it is a short distance from reproduction to fakery. The purpose of this type of finishing is to attempt to make the wood into something that it is not, and has no place in this book.

Finishing is a very personal process and one that has no hard and fast rules. Each maker must arrive at a system that suits them and their work, and it may continue to evolve through the remainder of their wood-working lives.

People love to stroke wood, especially in chairs, and any finish should have a texture that gives them the feeling that they are touching the wood directly.

It is not necessary to attend long courses to arrive at a system, unless a particular method (for example French polishing) is being taught. Windsor chairs have virtually no flat surfaces, and this feature offers challenges of its own that may not be present in case furniture. My advice is to read as much as possible on the subject, and to continue to experiment until you find a method that suits you. With the above proviso I will share with you several methods that have served me well over the years.

Preparation

Whatever the final finish, the surface must first be well prepared. As previously described, a cabinet scraper will remove small irregularities in the surface, and any roughness caused by the scraping can be removed rapidly with abrasives.

Three grades of abrasive should be sufficient at this stage for a Windsor chair: 120, 180 and 240 grit. The 120 grit should only ever be used in line with the grain, otherwise distinct marks will be left across the grain. Use a pad to spread the pressure on the wood and to increase the contact area. A pad also protects your hands, particularly on a lathe where heat build-up may be very rapid. Pads can be made of many things, but closed cell foam, as found in camping mats, is a great insulator and lasts for many months of hard use.

Many of the component parts should have been well sanded before their incorporation into the chair. For example, the seat and the legs should be fully sanded before being put together. Final sanding of the seat will be necessary once the leg tenons have been trimmed off the top surface, but only in patches rather than over the complete surface. It is much easier to sand an individual piece than the same piece assembled into the final chair: the other parts interfere, and it is difficult to access all the surfaces.

For maximum effect, the grain should be raised and sanded off before changing to the next, finer grit of abrasive. This approach works very well with the seat. A damp cloth passed over the surface should be sufficient, and if sanding outside on a breezy day, the place where you began with the damp cloth should be almost dry by the time you have dampened the remainder of the seat. If you spent five minutes initially with 120 grit, then the second sanding after dampening should take no more than sixty seconds. Repeat this for each grit to achieve a smooth surface.

Wet-sanding of turnings achieves the same effect with the minimum of effort. The grain is raised by drying the wet (sanded) legs, rather than wetting the already dry wood of the seat. A final very brief use of 240-grit paper on the dry turnings leaves a beautifully smooth surface.

Bows and arms will also benefit from grain-raising, though as already mentioned my preference is not to touch spindles with abrasives at all if they were shaved rather than turned.

Sealing the Wood

Having invested time in sanding, why not apply the finish straightaway? The risk is that the wood will absorb the finish unevenly, and the grain may be raised yet again, leaving a surface that is not as smooth as desired. Sealing solves both problems because it evens out absorption, and allows for yet more smoothing. Do not be tempted to miss out this process: it is quick and easy, and makes a disproportionate improvement to the finish compared with the effort expended.

Many proprietary products are available for sealing wood, and the most common is sanding sealer. This can be based on acrylic or shellac, and usually contains prodigious amounts of talc to help smooth the surface and fill pores. Unfortunately the surface that remains after sanding tends to have lost some of its 'life' due to the talc, and if sanding has not been sufficient, a distinct layer will remain, which is obvious and unattractive.

French polish (shellac) makes an excellent sealer on its own. If you are using a pale wood such as ash, then use a pale or transparent polish, whereas if using a darker wood such as oak or elm, then a darker polish such as Garnet Polish will add warmth to the wood, which may be desirable. There is no need to buy flakes and make up your own polish as you will not be using a great deal, and the dilution is not critical. A proprietary brand will work fine.

Dilute the polish by approximately 50 per cent with alcohol (for example, methylated spirits) and wipe it over every sur-

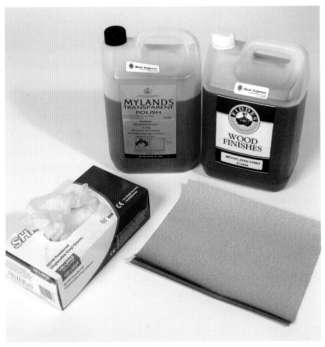

French polish, methylated spirits and 500-grit paper.

Apply dilute French polish all over the chair.

Sand all over with 500-grit paper.

face of the chair with a clean, lint-free rag. Work in a well ventilated room, or outside if the weather is warm and dry. Try not to leave runs or puddles, and make sure that each part has been wetted once; particularly ensure that all end grain has been wetted. Then leave the chair to dry: this should take less than five minutes in a warm environment.

Once dry, the surfaces will have become rough again as the grain will have been raised by the drying of the shellac. The amount of roughness will depend on how well the wood has previously been sanded. Rub the whole chair down with 500-grit paper, and this should produce a wonderfully smooth and silky surface. Half a sheet should be enough for a side chair.

Staining

This is the moment to stain the wood, if desired. Unfortunately, as I have already stated, most stained chairs look just that – stained. Unless you are very clever at colouring a chair and can replicate the changes brought about by age, then I would avoid the process.

My preference is to leave the wood in its natural state, unless it is fumed.

Fuming Wood

Woods that contain tannin, such as oak and sweet chestnut, can be quickly darkened with ammonia. The darkening can be controlled by adjusting the length of exposure, and it looks natural and does not in any way lessen the attractiveness of the grain; indeed, many people feel that it enhances the grain patterns.

Although liquid ammonia can be painted on to these tannin-containing woods, fuming is better. Place the chair inside a container and put a saucer containing concentrated ammonia solution (880 strength) on the floor. Diffusion will quickly fill the container with ammonia fumes, and the wood will begin to darken.

Great care is required with the ammonia solution, with gloves and eye protection being the absolute minimum protective clothing. It is advisable to do this outdoors, preferably on a windy day keeping the wind behind you so as to blow fumes away from your nose and eyes. The product is a strong

alkali. Follow all precautions advised by the supplier.

A container can be quickly made. Build a lightweight frame that will cover the chair, and cover it with clear polythene. Drawing pins are sufficient provided that joints are overlapped to prevent escape of the fumes.

Ten minutes of fuming makes a noticeable difference to oak, though for maximum effect leave the chair overnight. During this time all the fumes will eventually leak from the container, and you will be left with very dark brown wood. There are no hard and fast rules: it is up to you to experiment!

Fuming Box

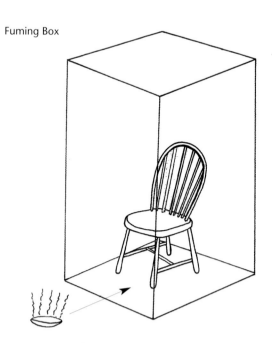

Oak and other tannin-containing woods can be darkened by fuming with ammonia. A plastic covered 'tent' is ideal for this. Place a bowl of ammonia inside the tent with the whole chair. This process is best undertaken outside.

Oil Finishes

Danish Oil is probably the most common oil finish applied to chairs. It is inexpensive and readily available, but is not ideal in my opinion. It is possible to get into trouble with it if you leave it for too long before wiping off the excess. It can become so sticky that wiping is no longer an option, and it must be mechanically removed before being reapplied. Also, the finish is too bright and hard for my taste.

I prefer to use a mixture that can be made up at home, made famous by the late Sam Maloof, maker of his iconic rocking chairs in California. The mixture is equal parts of boiled linseed oil, tung oil, and polyurethane gloss varnish. Although there are many similarities to Danish Oil, this mixture will take hours before it becomes too stiff to wipe off, and the final surface will not be as bright as Danish Oil. If you spill some on your bench and leave it to dry, it will remain flexible, whereas Danish Oil will dry hard like varnish.

Apply the oil generously with a rag. Then take a fresh rag and wipe as much oil as possible off the chair. It may be worth repeating this wiping with a second fresh cloth to ensure that absolutely no oil is left on the surface. Check the whole chair by walking around it looking for shiny surfaces, and rewipe if necessary. The surface should feel dry to the touch, although slightly waxy.

A second coat of oil is beneficial to producing a pleasing surface. This can take place within an hour of the first coat, or at any time afterwards. Further coats can be applied beyond the second – wiping off just as thoroughly each time – if you prefer to build up a thin layer; however, two is normally sufficient.

> **SPONTANEOUS COMBUSTION**
>
> When using any oil finish take great care that discarded rags do not self-combust. Heat is generated from the polymerization of the oil in the rags, and if it is compressed and perhaps surrounded by other insulating rubbish, the temperature can build up sufficiently for it to ignite.
>
> Although it is untidy, I tend to spread out each oily rag on the ground outside until it has hardened (a sign that the oil has polymerized). Alternatively place rags in a water-filled container. Whatever you do, do not bundle them up and throw them in a bin.

After about a week the oil will have cured, and the surface will lose its waxy feel. At this point apply a coat of furniture polish, and repeat as often as desired. There is no doubt that polishing will cause a chair to mellow and develop a patina of its own. Dark polishes will speed this process, but be careful of applying them to light-coloured woods such as ash, because the pigment will collect in the pores, exaggerating the grain patterns.

This oil finish should take no more than one and a half hours to apply, including the sealing process. If a chair takes, say, fifteen hours to make, then this seems a reasonable extra effort for all the benefits that it will give.

Finishing materials used after sealing wood.

Wipe on finish.

Linseed Wax

Recently I discovered this alternative to oil finishes described above. The mixture of linseed oil and beeswax can be simply wiped on with a rag after sealing the wood.

Work the wax well into the wood, and then with a dry cloth rub off every last trace of wax from the surface. The oil/wax mixture will be absorbed into the surface of the wood, and after a couple of treatments an attractive sheen will develop.

The finish will cure fully after about a week, and give the chair a good resistance to water marking. Occasional rewaxing will improve the look of the chair, although stop using it once the product is no longer absorbed into the wood; at this point a conventional furniture polish is a better choice.

Over time the linseed oil will encourage the wood to darken. I consider this to be a good thing, but avoid linseed oil if darkening is a problem. Pure tung oil will minimize this effect.

The wax is also an excellent product to use on oiled chairs.

Painting

MILK PAINTS

Painting chairs is common and popular in America, but is generally considered eccentric and undesirable in the UK. This is a shame, as all the earliest Windsor chairs were painted, but the tradition soon died out in England. Whatever your opinion, I think painting is something that all chairmakers should try at least once.

Originally chairs were painted with lead-based paints, but these are no longer available due to the toxicity of lead. One alternative today is to use milk paints which are made of lime, milk protein (casein) and earth pigments for colour. These are water-based and completely non-toxic.

Compared with oil-based paints these are quite different and require a completely different approach. They are more like a very thin, coloured plaster that could be applied to walls rather than chairs. They can be applied quickly and crudely, or with considerable care to produce sensual and attractive surfaces where the grain of the underlying wood shows through.

They can also be applied in contrasting layers and rubbed through, to simulate the repainting and wear that old chairs have often been subjected to. There is no need to seal the wood for milk paint, as the first coat achieves the same result.

Milk paints can be purchased as powders, or ready mixed in a can. The range of colours is very wide, but a finish of black over red will be described here.

Mix up the red paint, using approximately equal quantities of powder and water. Add the water to the powder in a lidded jar, and shake or swirl for approximately sixty seconds. Use a small dowel to remove any unmixed powder (look underneath the jar), and shake or swirl for a second minute. Then leave for at least sixty minutes, swirling or stirring occasionally.

With an artificial brush, apply the first coat. Apply it quickly and generously, but without leaving runs or puddles of paint.

Once dry, sand the whole chair with used 240-grit paper. This will remove the powdery surface and any grain that has been raised, forcing paint powder into the pores of the wood, and leaving a very smooth surface. This first coat and the subsequent rubbing down is equivalent to the sealing/sanding process described for the oil finish.

Apply a second coat of red. This time apply it carefully to produce an even layer. It is better to reload the brush frequently, rather than over-load it initially and then allow it to run dry. Try to maintain a constant load in the brush.

Allow to dry, then rub down with 0-grade wire wool.

Repeat with a third coat of red, rubbing down with 0-grade wire wool and burnishing with paper towel. If you are not happy with the resulting surface, another coat of red can be

Milk-paint powder and linseed paints (liquid).

applied, but otherwise continue to the next step.

Mix the black paint (approximately 50 per cent concentration of the red).

Carefully paint on the black paint, achieving the most even coverage possible, with a second thin coat if desired.

Rub through the black paint to the underlying red in the places where the surface would naturally wear (for example the seat, the front surface of the front legs, the bow). Use worn 500-grit paper very lightly to achieve the rub-through, doing less rather than more. The red will be more obvious once a finish has been applied. Continue to rub down with 0-grade wire wool, followed by 0000, and finally burnish with paper towel. The surface should now be smooth.

Evenly apply a coat of garnet French polish, using a brush or a rubber.

When the French polish is fully dry, take 0000 wire wool and clear furniture polish, such as linseed wax (as lubricant), and rub down the surface. Vigorous rubbing with plenty of polish will smooth out any unevenness in the shellac.

Rub off the remaining polish with a clean rag and burnish with a cloth.

If everything has gone well, the surface should be very smooth, and the underlying grain of the wood should be visible in places. Other colours can be used either on their own or in combination. Take care not to change the colour of the paint unintentionally by using dark French polish: use transparent polish if in any doubt.

French polish gives a very smooth final surface and brings out the colours better than using oil as a sealant, but it will be susceptible to water marking. If this is a likely hazard then use oil or linseed wax in place of French polish.

Milk paint is not a quick finishing option, unless it is applied thickly in one or two coats and allowed to age with use. However, there is no need or point in using expensive woods for the seat if painting is planned, and this economy can partly offset the time taken in finishing.

Elm (seat) and oak sack-back painted with milk paints (black over red) and sealed with French polish.

LINSEED PAINTS

These paints are a great alternative to milk paints. The original paints used on old chairs also used linseed oil as a medium. There is a wide range of attractive colours available, which rivals the scope of milk paints.

The biggest disadvantage of these paints is that they take a long time to dry – twenty-four hours at 20°C. However, two coats are probably sufficient, and the dry surface is virtually waterproof. These paints are applied with a brush, and spread more evenly than milk paints.

Chairmaking tools that need to be kept sharp include the following:

- Side axe
- Froe
- Drawknife
- Spokeshave
- Travisher
- Gouge
- Chisel
- Adze

- Scrub plane
- Block plane
- Jointer plane
- Roughing gouge
- Parting tool
- Skew chisel
- Spindle gouge

Sharpening

Sharpening is a process that must be mastered before any serious woodworking can be undertaken. Few tools are bought ready sharpened, and in any event they will soon need to be resharpened.

Whatever the method you settle on, it must be quick and effective, otherwise you won't do it frequently enough and your tools will only occasionally be sharp. Many books have been written on this subject alone, but as with so much in woodworking, the best system for you will depend on the type of work that you do, and will be developed after hours of reading and experimentation.

Windsor chairmaking involves the use of a wide range of edge tools that must all be kept sharp. However, the precise shape of the edges is not nearly as critical as in other disciplines such as cabinet making, where they must be square and straight in order to make joints effectively. The only situation where this is true in Windsor chairmaking is when sharpening a plane for jointing arms and blocks to make hands. In this case two flat surfaces must be created to produce a strong glue joint, and anything but a straight plane edge will be unsuccessful. Otherwise the tools are for shaping only.

If there is one sentence at the heart of my approach to sharpening it is this: 'A sharp edge is the intersection of two polished surfaces.' The critical word in this sentence is 'polished'. There is no mention of grinding, squareness or angles, which can all be added to a definition or system if desired, but get two polished surfaces to intersect and you will have a sharp edge.

Creating/ Modifying a Bevel by Grinding

In order to shape the bevel of a tool you will need to remove metal by grinding. Several tools can be used for this purpose and I use three for different situations. A bench grinder with ruby or white wheels will remove metal very quickly, and the special wheels will reduce, though not eliminate, the risk of blueing the metal. A slower, and more controlled tool is a water-cooled grindstone such as the Tormek. Blades can be held in a jig to set a precise angle, and the water cooling eliminates all risk of overheating. For larger tools such as axes and drawknives, a bench-mounted belt sander fitted with a 100-grit belt is a great tool for grinding.

Curved blades, with the bevel on the inside of the curve, present an interesting challenge when it comes to grinding. A drum sander fitted on to a pillar drill is very effective provided it is held carefully to avoid catching. Begin with a coarse abrasive such as 80 grit and work up to, say, 240 grit before polishing.

I grind all my tools freehand apart from plane blades, which I hold in the Tormek jig. This may sound a little cavalier, but it works! In my experience the sharpness of the edge is more important than the shape of the bevel. If you find that the blade is chipping after use, then the angle of the bevel is too small and a steeper bevel is required. If, when the tool is sharp, it takes too much effort to cut through the wood, then try lowering the bevel angle.

Some tools require a rounded bevel, and this can easily be produced by freehand grinding. Grinding should be done as little as possible because the process removes metal from your

Grinding stone in a water bath prevents overheating.

Sharpening a roughing gouge on a belt sander.

tool and shortens its life. In practice, unless tools are used professionally day in, day out, their lifespan is very long and can almost be discounted. If you insist on grinding the tool every time you sharpen it, you may suddenly find that your favourite tool is worn out and needs replacing. Grinding takes time, and it also lengthens the time needed to polish the surface. Time is precious, so do not waste it unnecessarily.

Turning tools can mostly be used direct from the grinder without polishing. This means that only the minimum of time is spent keeping them sharp. If sharpening is quick and easy it will be done regularly, rather than when the tool is completely blunt.

Turners usually have a bench grinder adjacent to the lathe for this job, while I have mounted my belt sander on top of the lathe bed for instant access. Roughing gouges and parting tools can be successfully sharpened this way, but in my experience skew chisels and spindle gouges need polishing to work at their best. In chairmaking most of the wood to be turned is wet, and therefore soft, and is cut readily by the somewhat ragged edge left by grinding. If you change your work pattern and begin to turn dry, harder wood, then polishing the bevels may become more important.

Polishing

Ignoring the exceptions mentioned above, this is when the sharpening actually takes place. The simplest method, requiring no machinery or electricity, is to polish the bevel with emery paper. This method was made popular by Mike Dunbar many years ago, and remains a supremely simple and effective method.

A range of emery paper from 500 grit to 2,000 grit is required, along with a glass plate and a ¾ in (19mm) diameter wooden dowel (say, 5in/13cm long).

In order to polish a flat surface such as the bottom of a wooden spokeshave blade, lay the emery paper on the glass plate, hold the flat surface on the paper, and rub backwards and forwards until the surface is worn all over. If the surface is seriously out of true, begin with, say, 320-grit paper until a uniformly flat surface is produced, then continue up the grits until a polished surface is achieved. The secret of this process is to apply a steady downward pressure on to the glass so there is no risk of the blade rocking, even slightly.

Flat surfaces are the easiest to polish, and everything can be done on the glass plate, but bevels are not so easily polished

TOOLS THAT WORK WELL WITH A ROUNDED BEVEL	
Froe	A splitting tool. The edge begins the split and subsequently plays no part. Must be thin enough to enter the wood and not bounce off.
Drawknife	Cross-section of blade should be like a knife (as in its name). Slightly steeper bevel on top and a shallow bevel on the lower surface.
Gouge	A rounded bevel allows you to work the edge into and out of the wood.
Adze	This tool will probably have a fairly straight bevel on top, but a small rounded bevel on the underside allows the blade to enter and exit the wood leaving a smooth, scalloped cut surface. If there is no bevel on the underside the tool will tend to bury itself deeper and deeper.
Roughing gouge	Many people hollow-grind a roughing gouge. I prefer a rounded bevel, which is produced naturally on a belt sander.
Skew chisel	Many people hollow-grind a skew chisel. I prefer a rounded bevel which is produced naturally on a belt sander.
Spindle gouge	A rounded bevel allows the tool to create attractive curves (coves) by following the curve of the bevel.

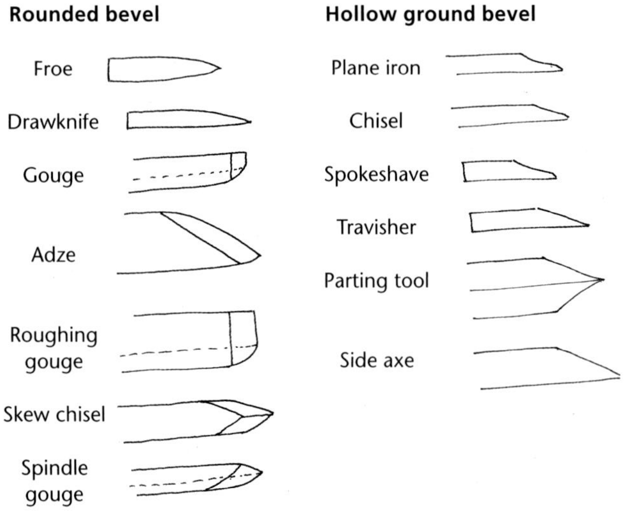

Rounded bevel

Froe

Drawknife

Gouge

Adze

Roughing gouge

Skew chisel

Spindle gouge

Hollow ground bevel

Plane iron

Chisel

Spokeshave

Travisher

Parting tool

Side axe

Some bevels should be flat and perhaps hollow ground, other tools will work better with a rounded bevel.

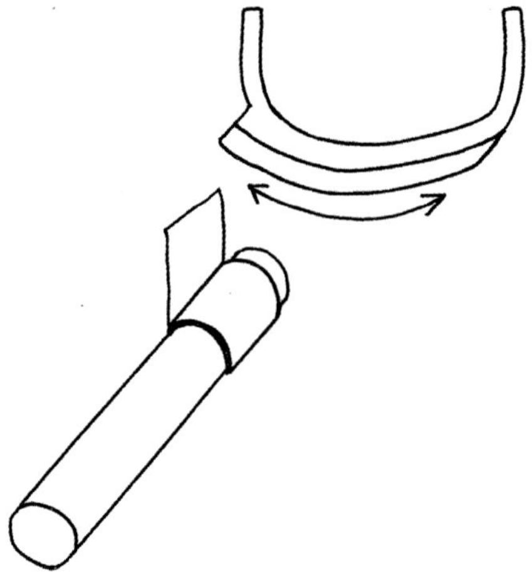

Curved blades can be successfully sharpened using a wooden dowel and a strip of emery paper wound around the end.

this way. Cut a slot in the top of the wooden dowel and tear emery paper of different grits into strips approximately 1in (2.5cm) wide. Slide one end of a strip into the slot and wind the paper around the stick. Hold the emery paper flat against the bevel (that is, at the correct angle) and begin to move it back and forth along the bevel. Rotate the stick slowly while rubbing along the bevel so that fresh paper is constantly being used, and tear off the worn-out paper as often as necessary.

When repolishing/resharpening, begin at 500 grit and work up to 2,000 or even 2,500 grit, but if the bevel has been ground and there are score marks to be removed first, then a coarser paper will be more appropriate to begin with (for example 320 grit).

This equipment can be carried around in a small box, and tools can be sharpened anywhere, independent of power and equipment. I always take my box to shows and other venues where I cannot be sure to have power.

Felt Wheels

One of the most efficient methods of polishing metal is to hold it against a spinning felt wheel loaded with abrasive. The edge of a wheel can travel very much further than a piece of emery paper on a stick in the same time. My felt-wheel polisher operates at 2,850rpm and has a 5in (13cm) diameter wheel. A point on the edge of the wheel travels almost 45,000in or 1,250 yards (1,145m) in one minute, while my emery paper on the dowel will travel no more than 1,200in (30m) in the same time when sharpening a 4in (10cm) spokeshave blade. Thus the edge of the wheel travels approximately thirty-six times further in the same time. This difference indicates the possibility of a much more rapid polishing method, and it is the one that I have adopted for virtually all the edge tools in my workshop.

Felt wheels are ideal for this job, with a hard and a softer wheel for straight and curved edges respectively. They must rotate away from the user, unlike a bench grinder where the wheels rotate towards the user. Attempting to use a felt wheel towards you is highly dangerous as the edge will almost certainly dig into the felt and be thrown towards you.

A standard bench grinder can be modified to hold felt wheels by reversing the guards and providing a readily acces-

sible switch (the original switch will now be at the back of the machine). Alternatively units are available set up for this purpose, or you can build your own.

The drawback of bench grinder-type units is that the motor housing can easily interfere with the tool to be polished. For example, the tangs of a spokeshave blade may touch the housing, preventing the bevel from being held flat against the wheel. Drawknife handles can also cause a similar problem.

Abrasives (known as 'soap' because they are supplied in bars) of varying coarseness are available for different materials. In my experience green and grey soaps are a good choice for this type of work. The bar is held against the edge of the spinning wheel for a moment to load the surface with abrasive, and then the bevel is applied to begin polishing.

The greatest drawback of this method is that it is easy to round over the bevel of the tool if care is not taken to hold it against the wheel at the correct angle. With practice this becomes second nature, however, and the amount of unintended rounding becomes minimal.

When held at the correct angle, liquid abrasive begins to appear in front of the blade as it is being sharpened. It will have a silvery appearance because it contains a small amount of metal from the blade. Considerable heat will build up, but it will become uncomfortable to the fingers before it can damage the blade. Once the bevel has been polished, the blade can be turned over and the back can be polished. If no bevel is desired, then hold it almost in line with the wheel (rather than at 90 degrees to the direction of spin), but at a slight angle so there is no chance of it digging in. This method uses just one (fine) abrasive to polish the metal, but the speed of the wheel means that even freshly ground bevels can be polished in a short time; and blades to be repolished will need only seconds to achieve a sharp edge.

I can sharpen the following tools in well under ninety minutes while removing only a tiny amount of metal:

- Sixteen spokeshaves
- Five drawknives
- Five adzes
- Five travishers
- Ten gouges
- Four chisels
- Five inshaves
- One scrub plane
- Two block planes

Sharpening a drawknife on felt wheels.

Loading a felt wheel with 'soap'.

This system is well suited for Windsor chairmaking tools, but will not be perfect for everybody but it is quick and easy, and takes away much of the mystique surrounding sharpening.

Measurement

Should one use imperial or metric units for measurement when making a Windsor chair? The obvious answer would be to follow the norm in your own country: thus metric in the UK and imperial in the USA – but perhaps politicians who decide national standards for measurements do not necessarily know much about making chairs. I would firmly suggest that you use imperial (that is, inches) most of the time. If I were stranded on a desert island with all the tools and materials for making Windsor chairs, but with no rules or tape measures, I would have to invent a scale for myself. To be useful it would inevitably be based on a unit similar to an inch and divided into eighths and possibly sixteenths. Surely a millimetre, which is finer (37 per cent less) than $\frac{1}{16}$in, would be more accurate and therefore better? In making a Windsor chair successfully very little has to be measured with great accuracy, and $\frac{1}{16}$in is close to the limit of accuracy that is required. This may sound like a 'country mile' to a cabinet maker, but it is really quite sufficient for chairs. The joints of Windsors are almost all round tenons in round holes.

The drill makes the mortice, and tenons can be made using a gauge drilled by the same bit. No need to measure a thing, except the depth of the mortice and length of the tenon. At other times the tenon is made over-size and driven into the hole – again no measurement, just a visual judgment of size relative to the hole.

In addition to the fineness of measurement, the imperial system was based around lengths of the human body, and since chairs are designed to support the human body, there is a natural association. For example the height of the seat is normally 17–18in above the ground, which is much easier to remember than 432–457mm.

In the end the choice is yours. If you feel the need to use a micrometer to measure everything, then fine; but just keep in the back of your mind that measuring to the nearest 1/16in is sufficient in most Windsor situations, and after a few chairs you may lay that micrometer down!

CHAPTER 4

TWO ENGLISH CHAIRS

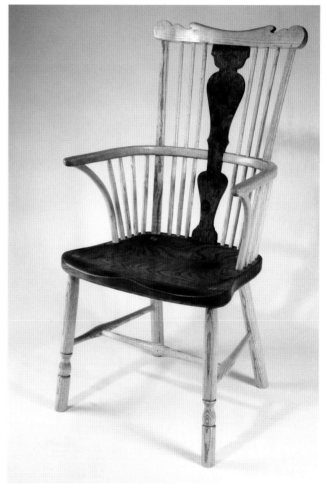

Chapters 4 and 5 give the information necessary to complete four quite different chairs. Most of the techniques required should be covered elsewhere in the book, but there is no guarantee that it is entirely comprehensive. Use the photographs of the chairs to gain clues and further information that you may need; most problems can be overcome with a little thought and improvisation, and do not be afraid to experiment and develop your own techniques.

The two chairs chosen for this chapter come from different periods of Windsor history. The design of the comb-back armchair dates from around 1760, while the wheelback chair is from around eighty years later. Both chairs exhibit the typical English characteristics of upright front legs and splats in their backs. The earlier splat is plain, while the later version is pierced in the well known form of a wheel. The seat shapes are very similar, even though their sizes are quite different and one is an armchair, and the other a side chair. The turnings are typical English patterns, but are completely different, coming from different periods.

The techniques required to make these chairs encompass most that are needed to make any English chair. The spindles ideally should be turned, or made with a trapping plane.

Shaving them will work, but they will have a slightly different character from the originals.

Use of Drawings

Scale drawings are given for seats and bending formers in Chapters 4 and 5. The easiest way of converting them to full size is to scan the pictures into a computer and then expand them to the exact size required. Any desktop publishing software (e.g. Microsoft Publisher) will be able to do this. Print the full size image and join several pieces of paper together with tape. Cut round the shape and you will have a useable template.

The wheelback chair – front and back.

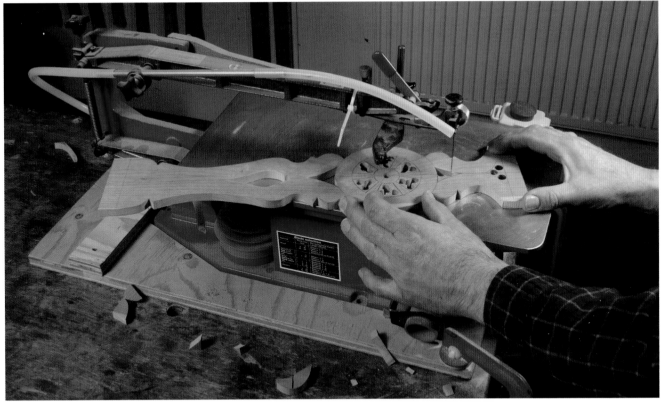

Cutting out the splat with a fretsaw.

The Wheelback Chair

This is one of the few nineteenth-century chairs in this book, but it earns its place by being an attractive and compact side chair with different constructional challenges to the comb-back chairs of the eighteenth century.

The pierced splat is best cut out with a mechanical fretsaw, but can be done by hand with care and patience. The splats of some old chairs had the edges of the splats cut at an angle so that the visual thickness of the splat was reduced when seen from the front. This is not essential, but adds finesse to the chair.

The tail extension behind the splat anchors two extra spindles that brace the back of the chair. These are inserted into the bow between the two outer spindles on each side. The holes in the seat can be drilled by aiming, using the same technique as for the other spindles, and the corresponding holes in the bow can be lined up using a piece of dowel or threaded rod, and drilled in exactly the same manner as the others, but at a rather different angle. These two extra spindles (and the 'tail') are not essential for the structure of the chair and can be omitted with no ill effect, but the extra structure adds to the visual impact of the chair.

The bow is quite thick, and an effort should be made to hide the thickness by careful spokeshaving of the straight arms that rise up from the seat. Slight tapering towards the back will make them appear thinner when seen from the front.

Drill the mortice for the splat using the same aiming technique as for the spindles.

Assemble the back of the chair first with the splat alone. Then remove the splat and drill the seat and bow for the spindles, and fit together. Finally assemble with the splat, but make sure that the splat does not prevent the bow from coming down fully over the spindles.

Wheel-back Data Sheet   measurements in inches unless otherwise stated

Blanks	QUANTITY	L	W	D
legs	4	20 ½	1 ⅞	1 ⅞
stretchers	3	17	1 ¾	1 ¾
seat	1	16 ½	16 ¼	1 ½ - 1 ¾
bow	1	54	1 ⅛	1
spindles	8	4 x 20 ¼; 2 x 19 ¾ 2 x 17 ½	⅞	⅞

Positions on Seat	FROM BACK	FROM CENTRE LINE	ANGLE (°)	DIAMETER
bottom of seat				
back legs	4 ¼	4 ¾	18	⅞
front legs	14 ¾	6 ¼	8	⅞
top of seat				
bow	5 ¾	5 ⅝	23	¾

Spindle Spacing	FROM CENTRE
seat	2 ½, 1 ⅛, 1 ⅛
bow (along top)	3 ⅝, 1 ⅝, 1 ⅞

Spindle Sizing	WET	MORTICE SIZE
top	11 mm	⅜
middle	14 -16 mm	
base	13 mm	⁷⁄₁₆

NB. diameter of centre of finished spindles is a matter of choice

Height

seat to top of bow	18 ¼

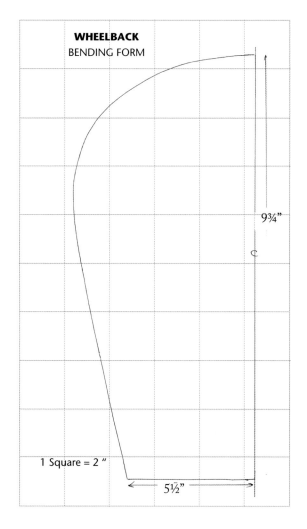

WHEELBACK
BENDING FORM

9¾"

1 Square = 2 "

5½"

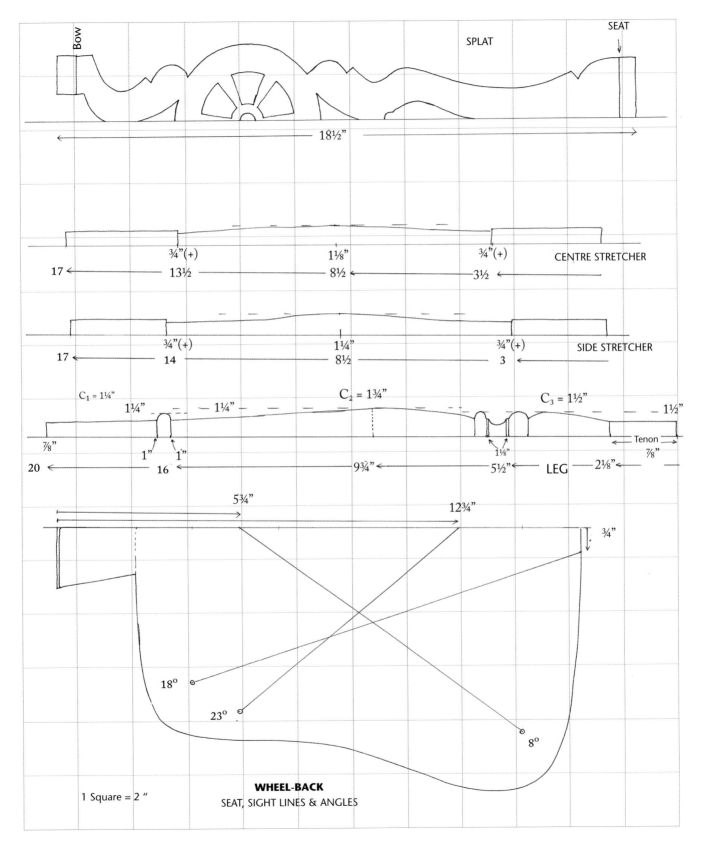

Bow

SPLAT

SEAT

18½"

¾"(+)   1⅛"   ¾"(+)   CENTRE STRETCHER

17 ←   13½   8½ ←   3½ ←

¾"(+)   1¼"   ¾"(+)   SIDE STRETCHER

17 ←   14   8½   3 ←

$C_1 = 1¼"$ $C_2 = 1¾"$ $C_3 = 1½"$

1¼"   — 1¼"   — 1½"

⅞"   Tenon

1"   1"   1⅛"   ⅞"

20 ←   16 ←   9¾" ←   5½" ←   LEG   2⅛" ←

5¾"

12¾"

¾"

18°

23°

8°

1 Square = 2 "

WHEEL-BACK
SEAT, SIGHT LINES & ANGLES

115

The Comb-back Chair

This is a complex chair involving many challenges. The addition of ribbon slats to the back, along with spindles and the splat, adds to the complications, but the end result is worth the effort. The 'stool' can be assembled in the normal way.

As the arm is held parallel to the seat, the blind mortices for the short spindles can be drilled on the tilting table using the sight lines and angles given. Do not forget to drill the short spindle mortices in the seat in the same way, while drilling for the legs and arm-posts.

With the splat mortised into the seat at 14 degrees, hold the arm at the correct height above the seat and mark the position of the splat on the front of the arm. Rebate the arm so that the splat fits snugly, leaving approximately ½in (13mm) of thickness behind the splat on the top of the arm.

Next mount the arm on to the short spindles at the correct height.

Drill the seat and the arm for the long spindles by aiming.

Mortice the crest to fit on to the splat.

Drill the crest to accept the spindles and slats, and fit all together.

Finally fit the curved arm-posts to fit to the arm.

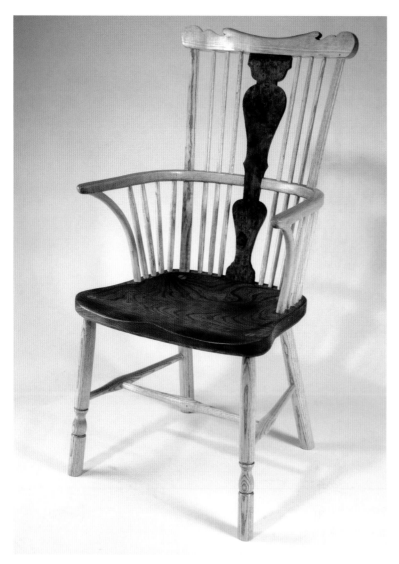

The English comb-back chair.

Views of the English comb-back chair.

Chair ready for cutting
mortices in the crest
for the ribbon slats,
and then fitting the
arm parts.

Arm fitted onto short
spindles and splat
morticed into the seat and
rebated into the arm.

Comb-back Data Sheet   measurements in inches unless otherwise stated

Blanks

	QUANTITY	L	W	D
legs	4	20 ½	2	2
side stretchers	2	18	1 ⅝	1 ⅝
centre stretchers	1	19	1 ⅝	1 ⅝
arm posts (makes2)	1	40	⅞	⅞
seat	1	17 ½	20	1 ¾ - 2
				NB Hands 7"long x 1¼" wide
arm	1	50 ½	1 ⅛ (+)	1 (+)
crest	1	22	1 ⅛ (+)	2 ¾
spindles-long	6	25 ½	⅞	⅞
spindles-short	8	12 ½	⅞	⅞
splat	1	23 ½	4 ¾	⅜ (+)
ribbon slats	2	25	1 ¼	⁷⁄₁₆

Positions on Seat

	FROM BACK	FROM CENTRE LINE	ANGLE (°)	
bottom of seat				
back legs	2 ½	5 ¾	17	⅞
front legs	14 ¾	8 ½	5	⅞
top of seat				
arm posts	7 ¾	8	10	¾

Spindle Spacing

	SEAT	ARM	CREST
centre	0	0	adjust all spacings by eye/ measurement to look good
spindle 1	2 ⅜	2 ⅝	
spindle 2	1 ⅛	1 ¼(+)	
spindle 3	1 ⅛	1 ¼(+)	
ribbon slat (1 ⅛" wide)	1 ⁷⁄₁₆	adjust positon of slat by eye	
short spindle	1 ⁷⁄₁₆	3 ¼	
short spindle	1 ¼	2	
short spindle	1 ¼	2	
short spindle	1 ¼	2	

Spindle Sizing

	wet	mortice size
top	11 mm	⅜
middle	14.5 mm	½
base	13 - 14 mm	⁷⁄₁₆

Angle of Splat in Seat   14 degrees

Heights

seat to base of arm	9
seat to base of crest in centre	22 ½

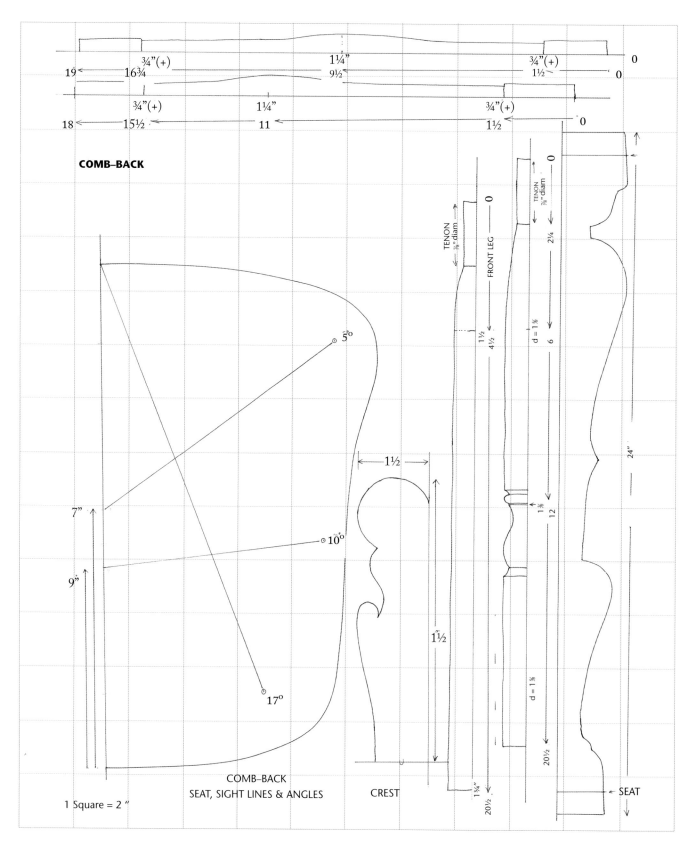

¾"(+)   1¼"   ¾"(+)   0

19 ← 16¾   9½ ←   1½ →   0

¾"(+)   1¼"   ¾"(+)

18 ← 15½ ←   11 ←   1½ ←   0

COMB–BACK

5°

7"

10°

9"

17°

TENON
⅞" diam

1½
4½

FRONT LEG ——— 0

TENON
⅞" diam

d = 1⅜

2¼

6

0

1½

1¼"

1⅜
12

1½

24"

d = 1⅜

20½

COMB–BACK
SEAT, SIGHT LINES & ANGLES

CREST

1¾"

20½

← SEAT

1 Square = 2 "

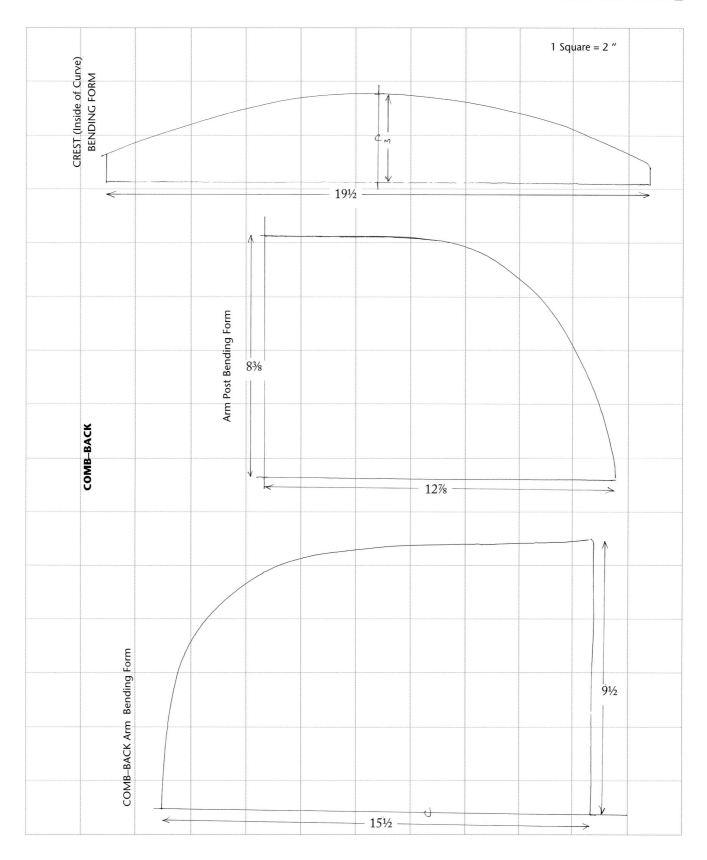

1 Square = 2 "

CREST (Inside of Curve)
BENDING FORM

3

19½

COMB-BACK

Arm Post Bending Form

8⅜

12⅞

COMB-BACK Arm Bending Form

9½

15½

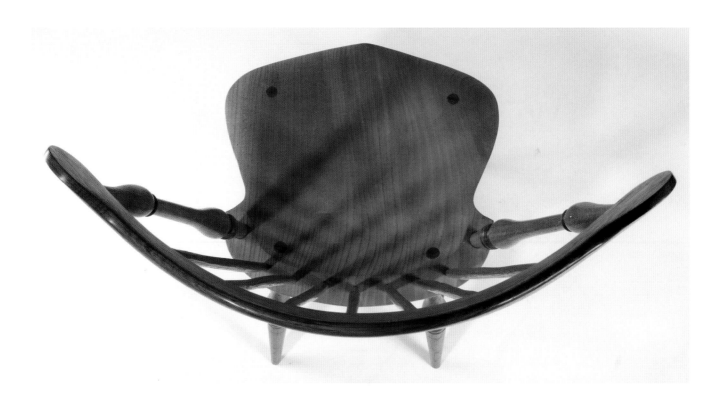

CHAPTER 5

TWO AMERICAN CHAIRS

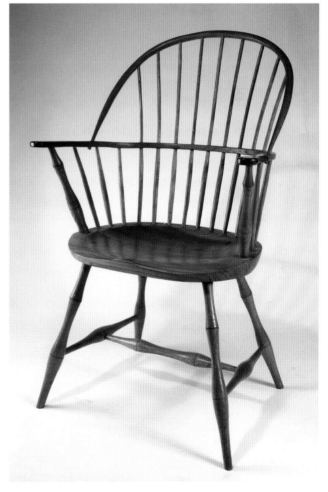

Both of these chairs, one with a crest and the other with a bent bow, exhibit the typical lightness and elegance of American chairs; their whole appearance is a contrast to their English cousins in the previous chapter. In both chairs the spindles should ideally be shaved with a drawknife and spokeshaves.

Views of the American fanback side chair.

The Fanback Side Chair

This fanback is a compact but very comfortable chair. It has deliberately been made with a slightly reduced splay to the front legs and back-posts in order to keep it compact. If you wish to make it appear a little more dramatic, then adjust the sight lines (and perhaps the angles slightly) of the front legs and back-posts – though if you change the back then check that the crest is still long enough.

The crest is quite thin, in keeping with the lightness of the chair, and the spindle mortices are just 5/16in, less than any of the other chairs. Make sure that the back-post turnings are kept light, otherwise the back will become heavy and the chair's elegance will be lost.

This is a relatively simple chair to make, and one that can be put together without the need for steam-bending, if the crest is laminated.

The American fanback side chair–rear view.

Fanback Data Sheet   measurements in inches unless otherwise stated

Blanks

	NUMBER	L	W	D	
legs	4	20 ½	2	2	
stretchers	3	3 x 18	1 ¾	1 ¾	
back posts	2	21	1 ¾	1 ¾	
seat	1	16 ⅛ (along grain)	17	1 ½	
crest	1	24	¾	2 ¼	
spindles	7	19	⅞	⅞	

Positions on Seat

		FROM BACK	FROM CENTRE LINE	ANGLE (°)	DIAMETER
bottom of seat	back legs	3	4 ½	14 ½	⅞
	front legs	12 ¾	5 ¾	12 ½	⅞
top of seat	back posts	4	6 ¾	14 ½	⅞

Spindle Spacing

seat	1 ¾
crest	2 ⅛

Spindle Sizing

	WET	MORTICE SIZE
top	⅜	⁵⁄₁₆
middle	personal choice	
base	⁹⁄₁₆	⁷⁄₁₆

Height

seat to bottom of crest	17	

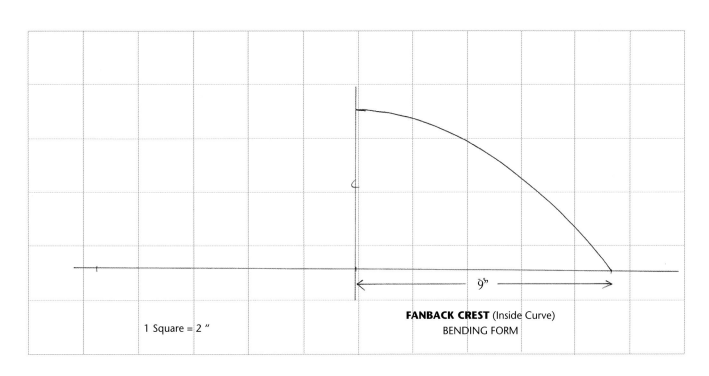

1 Square = 2 "

9"

FANBACK CREST (Inside Curve)
BENDING FORM

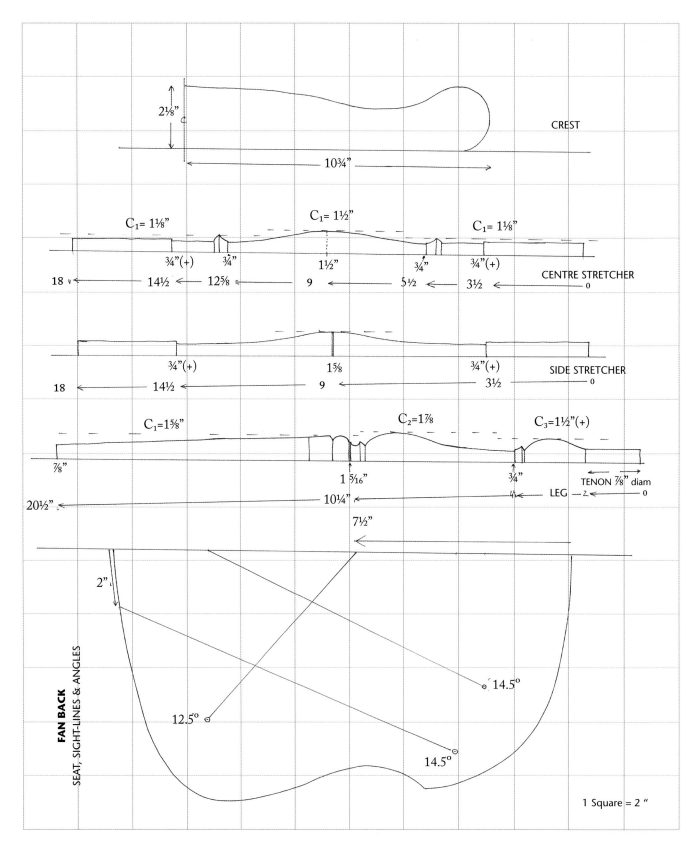

CREST

2⅛"

10¾"

C_1= 1⅛" C_1= 1½" C_1= 1⅛"

CENTRE STRETCHER

¾"(+)   ¾"   1½"   ¾"   ¾"(+)

18   14½   12⅝   9   5½   3½   0

SIDE STRETCHER

¾"(+)   1⅝   ¾"(+)

18   14½   9   3½   0

C_1=1⅝" C_2=1⅞ C_3=1½"(+)

⅞"   1 5/16"   ¾"   TENON ⅞" diam

LEG   2   0

20½"   10¼"   4½   0

7½"

2"

14.5°

12.5°

14.5°

FAN BACK
SEAT, SIGHT-LINES & ANGLES

1 Square = 2 "

126

The Double-bow Chair

This large double-bow chair can be used up to a table or alone. The nine long spindles will take plenty of work if you are not familiar with making spindles, but the curves of their upper (thinner) sections, which result from fitting between the arm and bow, make the chair interesting to look at, as well as comfortable.

The bamboo-style turnings are some of the simplest available, but the simplicity in no way detracts from the chair. As an alternative the style of turnings from the fanback could be substituted.

This chair is a wonderful project on which to perfect the art of 'aiming' the drill. There are fifty-five holes to be drilled altogether, and all but six are drilled freehand.

Views of the American double–bow chair.

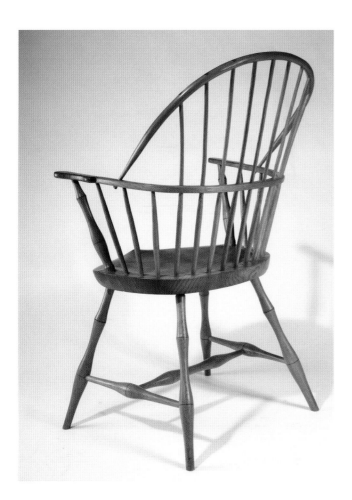

Sack Back Data Sheet   measurements in inches unless otherwise stated

Blanks	NUMBER	L	W	D	
legs	4	20 ½	2	2	
side stretchers	2	18	2	2	
centre stretchers	1	21	2	2	
arm posts	2	13 ½	1 ¾	1 ¾	
seat	1	21	16 ¾	1 ¾	
arm	1	52	⅞	⅝	
bow	1	52	⅞	⅞	
long spindles	9	3 x 24; 2 x 23; 2 x 22; 2 x 21	⅞	⅞	
short spindles	6	6 x 11 ¾	⅞	⅞	

Positions on Seat		FROM BACK	FROM CENTRE LINE	ANGLE (°)	DIAMETER
bottom of seat	back legs	3 ⅜	5 ½	23	⅞
	front legs	12 ¼	7	18	⅞
top of seat	arm posts	9 ¾	9 ½	23	⅞

Spindle Spacing	LONG	SHORT		
seat	1 ¾	1 ¾		
arm	2	2 ¾; 3 ¼; 3 ¾		
bow	2 ⅝; 2 ¾; 2 ⅞; 2 ⅞			

Spindle Sizing	WET	MORTICE SIZE		
top	10.5 mm	⅜		
shoulder	11.5 mm	10.5 mm	NB. diameter @ 9 ⅝" from base of spindle	
base	⅝	½		

NB. diameter of centre of finished spindles is a matter of choice

Height   Seat to top of bow   22
Seat to bottom of arm behind armposts   9
Seat to bottom of arm at centre spindle   8 ½

Angle of bow to arm   38 ½ °

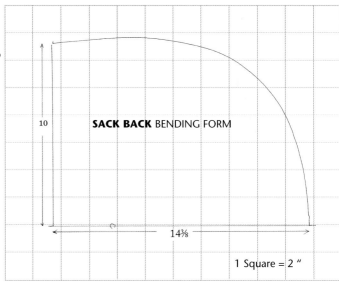

10

SACK BACK BENDING FORM

14⅜

1 Square = 2 "

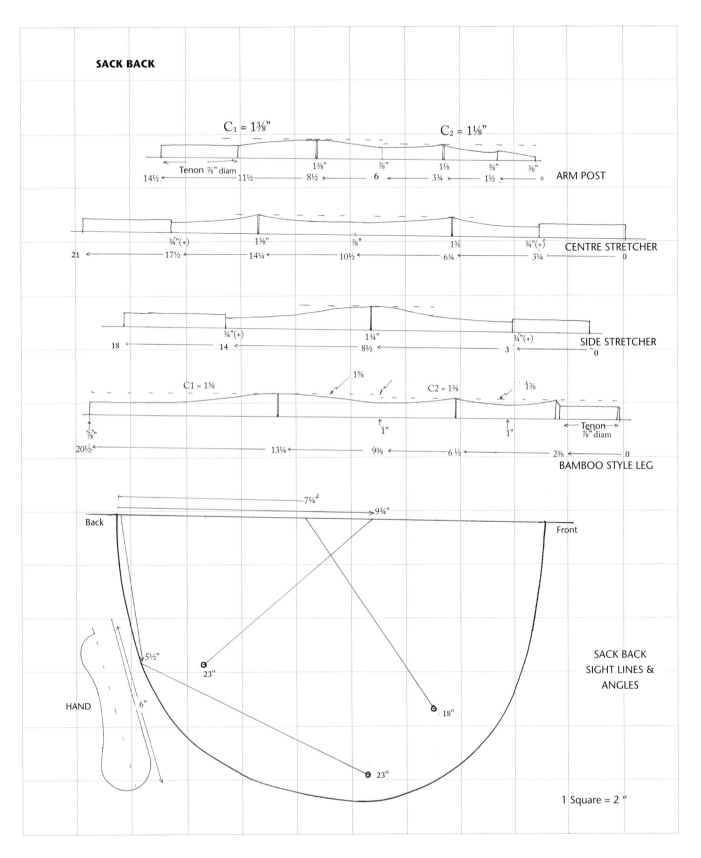

SACK BACK

$C_1 = 1\frac{3}{8}"$ $C_2 = 1\frac{1}{8}"$

Tenon ⅞" diam $1\frac{3}{8}"$ $\frac{7}{8}"$ $1\frac{1}{8}"$ $\frac{5}{8}"$ $\frac{3}{8}"$

$14\frac{1}{2}$ $11\frac{1}{2}$ $8\frac{1}{2}$ 6 $3\frac{3}{4}$ $1\frac{1}{2}$ 0   ARM POST

$\frac{3}{4}"(+)$ $1\frac{3}{8}"$ $\frac{7}{8}"$ $1\frac{3}{8}$ $\frac{3}{4}"(+)$

21   $17\frac{1}{2}$ $14\frac{1}{4}$ $10\frac{1}{2}$ $6\frac{3}{4}$ $3\frac{1}{4}$ 0   CENTRE STRETCHER

$\frac{3}{4}"(+)$ $1\frac{3}{4}"$ $\frac{3}{4}"(+)$

18   14 $8\frac{1}{2}$ 3   0   SIDE STRETCHER

$C1 = 1\frac{5}{8}$ $1\frac{5}{8}$ $C2 = 1\frac{3}{8}$ $1\frac{3}{8}$

$\frac{7}{8}"$ $1"$ $1"$ Tenon ⅞" diam

$20\frac{1}{2}$ $13\frac{1}{4}$ $9\frac{3}{8}$ $6\frac{1}{2}$ $2\frac{3}{8}$ 0   BAMBOO STYLE LEG

$7\frac{1}{4}"$

$9\frac{3}{4}"$

Back   Front

$5\frac{1}{2}"$

23°

HAND $6"$

18°

23°

SACK BACK
SIGHT LINES &
ANGLES

1 Square = 2 "

CHAPTER 6

LESSONS FROM THE PAST

A little while ago I was given the opportunity to study a classic Thames Valley comb-back Windsor armchair. This chair must be one of the better known Windsors in existence, being pictured on the dustjacket of certain editions of Dr Bernard 'Bill' Cotton's *The English Regional Chair*. It quickly became apparent that there was much more to be recorded than just measurements.

The maker of this chair left a wonderfully detailed record of how it had been made by leaving his tool marks clearly visible in many places. As a maker, I was able to recognize many marks that I regularly make on chairs, and to empathize with this maker, understanding some of the challenges that he faced while making the chair. Not only was it possible to interpret the tool marks left on the chair, but also to speculate on the methods of production based on evidence in the chair, and to explore the maker's philosophy.

Construction

Seat

The elm seat is 24in (60cm) wide by 17¾in (45cm) deep across the grain. The board probably came from a plank adjacent to the centre board when the tree was sawn through and through. This is often the widest usable board in the tree because the centre board will have a crack along the line of the pith caused by the deformation, by shrinkage, of the tightly curved rings at the centre. Viewed from the side of the seat, the tightly curved rings can be seen under the arm-post and first short spindle, while they become close to vertical (quarter-sawn) as one moves to the front and back of the seat.

Endgrain of seat showing annual rings most curved between the arm-post and the first short spindle. The hollow of the curve of the grain faces upwards.

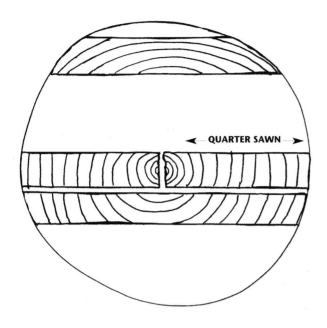

The seat was cut from the plank adjacent to the centre board. This would bave been one of the two widest useable boards as the centre board is always split due to the presence of the split.

Scrub plane marks on the underside of the seat in the central section. No plane marks at the front and back of the seat.

On drying, such a board would be expected to cup away from the centre of the tree, because the wood shrinks more along the rings than across them, and this difference is magnified at the centre of the plank where the wood is cut radially at the top, and tangentially at the bottom. However, this chair is deeply cupped in the opposite direction. On the underside one can see deep scrub plane marks where the maker has made an effort to reduce the crowning. The marks are deepest in the area where the rings are most tightly curved, but there are no marks close to the front and back of the seat where the rings are almost vertical in the seat.

This unexpected deformation probably came about from working on a partly seasoned board. The hollowing on the seat is very deep – a maker might describe this as brave – leaving only ½in (13mm) of thickness over a considerable area of the seat blank, which is 1⅞in (47mm) thick at the edge. If the board were not fully seasoned – that is, was not in equilibrium throughout the thickness – then hollowing would have exposed wetter wood, which would subsequently have dried, curling the seat towards the top surface.

The unsculpted top surface of the seat along each side does not show this deformation, so it is likely that the maker would have planed the top surface reasonably flat before drilling and

assembling the chair. In fact the thickness at the front is 1¾in (44mm), supporting this theory. The thickness at the back was not measured. The top surface may, however, have remained relatively flat because of the opposing forces in action, in that normal drying causes cupping down, and hollowing a damp seat causes cupping up.

If the movement of the wood took place after the chair was assembled, then one would have expected to see that it had been pulled apart and subsequently repaired. However, in my experience such movement occurs during and immediately after hollowing. Also, if the movement had happened after assembly there would have been no need, or opportunity, to use the scrub plane. The evidence of the scrub plane marks confirms that the movement took place prior to construction.

The hollowing of the seat is unusual in that it is concave from the back almost to the very front edge. This produces an even more capacious seat than the great width (24in/60cm) would suggest. It also has the effect of lightening the chair both visually and in weight. Most Windsor seats become convex a few inches from the front edge in order to avoid a sharp edge cutting into the bottom of the sitter's thigh. However, this does not seem to be a problem in this chair.

Not only did the maker expend a lot of energy hollowing

Side of seat shaped in a gentle curve.

Rough chamfer along the lower edge of the seat.

the seat, but he also took the trouble to put a decorative bead around the side and back edge, drawing attention away from the thickness of the seat. In addition to this, the sides have been bevelled inwards around all the edges, and a rough chamfer has been applied around the bottom, both processes contributing to a visual lightening of the seat.

Many later chairs have vertical sides to their seats, requiring the minimum of work, but this maker must have considered the shaping very important because rounding the end grain of elm is hard work! The shaping was obviously considered more important than the finishing because there are clear striations visible across the end grain produced almost certainly by a blade, probably a spokeshave, with nicks in the edge. Also the chamfer at the base is very roughly made, varying considerably in width over short distances, and still rough in finish. The appearance suggests that it was made with a coarse tool such as a drawknife.

The Spindles

The chair has eight short, and six long spindles. The spindles are at first glance uniform, but closer inspection shows enormous variation in thickness and profile. They have also warped considerably, particularly the long spindles, some of which are far from straight.

Considerable debate surrounds the way that English spindles were made. These were obviously hand made due to the variation, but also because the tapering is attractively but not identically done, particularly on the long spindles above the arm. Neither of these features would have been achieved using an automated machine, which would have been quite out of keeping with the flavour of the rest of the chair, and probably quite unrealistic at the time this chair was made, between c. 1740 and 1770.

There is direct evidence that at least the short spindles were turned on a lathe. The photograph shows striations running perpendicular to the axis of the short spindle typical of those produced by turning. These marks are on the outside of the chair in a position likely to receive minimal wear. In addition to these marks, the base of the fourth spindle from the front, on the right-hand side, which is visible from below, has a dim-

Variation in shape of short spindles.

Evidence of turning on short spindles.

ple consistent with that made by the tailstock of a lathe.

The profiles and variation of the long spindles are completely consistent with them having been turned on the lathe. Another reason to suggest turning rather than shaving is that the grain is not straight, and in fact runs out at various points along the length of some of the long spindles. The unevenness of the grain may have caused them to warp as they dried fully. If they were turned it is quite possible, and even likely, that a spokeshave or abrasive would have been used to clean up the tool marks left by the turning tool.

The spindles were driven into the seat from the top, sometimes coming all the way through to the bottom. Tenons were formed by shaving the bottoms of the spindles, probably with a drawknife. The evidence for this can be seen just above seat level, where flat facets taper down to the hole. This is clearly visible on the long spindles. The flatness of the facets suggests that they were made with a flat blade, and their length (in some cases at least 2in/5cm) suggests a drawknife. The alternative tool would be a flat chisel, but it would be difficult to control the cut over such a distance.

Dimple in the base of a short spindle, probably from the tailstock of the lathe.

Non-straight grain of spindles precludes shaving.

At the back of the fifth long spindle from the left, the clean facets have been disfigured, presumably to improve the shape or fit, by a tool such as a rasp. Almost certainly this is the same tool that was used on the inside of the cabriole legs (see below).

The holes in the seat appear to have been drilled with a round-nosed bit, such as a spoon bit. This is evidenced by the fact that all the holes come through to the base of the seat, but the opening on the underside is of varying diameter. Where there is only a small hole, the internal diameter of the hole very rapidly reaches its full width, consistent with a round-nosed bit just breaking the surface of the underside.

The combination of the faceted tenon biting into the walls of the mortice, and the tenon extending through the full thickness of the seat, gives an extremely secure anchorage for the spindle. This method of fixing could not be tested before final assembly. The spindle would have been driven home once, and once only. This shows complete confidence in drilling the seat holes at the correct angles, or at least close enough for the flexibility of the spindle to allow assembly.

Faceted tenons on the base of spindles;

Note the rasp marks.

The Cabriole Legs

The front legs are made of yew, and the rear pair of ash. On inspecting them just above the seat, it was noticed that none of the blocks from which the legs were formed were accurately square. They have all been crudely shaped, with no attempt made to remove the tool marks.

There are no signs of saw marks on the inside faces. It seems likely that the blanks were cleft from green wood, and roughly squared up with a drawknife and planes, so accounting for the lack of precision in producing a right angle. If this was the case, then much of the shaping might have been carried out while the wood was still green and soft, with the finishing done when it had dried.

There are very clear rasp marks just below the 'square' section. The lower leg was finished with a spokeshave (slight facets can be seen with the naked eye with an angled light), but only up as far as the spokeshave could comfortably travel before interfering with the 'square' section. No effort was made to remove the rasp marks from the concave surfaces on the backs of the legs.

On one of these 'square' faces of the front right-hand leg, looking from the front, there is evidence of a knot having fallen out of the wood. This might have occurred as the blank dried and the knot shrank and then fell out.

The corner block attached to the front left leg shows signs of having been shaped with a rasp in situ, while attached to the leg. The rasp marks are continuous across the leg and block. Presumably this represented final detailed shaping, and care was taken to remove most of the visible rasp marks.

Finally, each cabriole leg shows signs of being hit with a hammer on the corner of the 'square' section, presumably to drive it into the seat mortices.

Evidence that cabriole legs were not square.

Rasp marks behind the knee of the cabriole leg.

Block on the side of the cabriole leg (from below), showing continuous rasp marks across the leg and block.

Block from the side.

Hammer mark on the cabriole leg.

The Arm

The arm is made of yew, and was bent as a whole branch. This can be deduced from the annual rings surrounding the hollow pith, and from the fact that moving away from the pith there is first the dark heartwood, and then the pale sapwood.

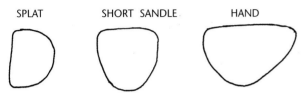

The arm is shaped in different ways along its length.

The arm has been carefully shaped along its length to leave the minimum amount of wood consistent with sufficient strength and the appropriate scale for such a significant chair. As with the finishing of the seat and legs, the shape has taken precedence over the finish. This can be judged by the flaws that were left on the arm at the hand and behind the ribbon splat. Some of these flaws were most likely present in the branch prior to bending, and were not considered reason enough to discard the completed bend, but others appear to be delaminations that have been snapped off incompletely, and then torn further.

Pre-existing flaw in the bow wood.

Pith visible at the end of each arm.

Slight delamination that has been partially snapped off from left to right and then torn off completely, leaving a further (smaller) scar.

Unsymmetrical splat.

Through-mortice for splat. Note the two faceted nail heads,
one with a scrap of label.

The Splat

The splat is made of yew, and appears to have been cut out by hand. While the effect is excellent, close examination shows that it is far from symmetrical. It is inserted into a mortice in the seat. This mortice continues through the full thickness of the seat, but tapers in thickness towards the bottom. The splat is ⅜in (9mm) thick at the top of the seat, but 3/16in (5mm) where it emerges from the bottom of the seat. The mortice is fairly accurately sized at the top, but ragged and ill-fitting at the bottom.

The Ribbon Slats

It should be noted that the ribbon slats are twisted by 15–20 degrees between the arm and the crest. It is difficult to imagine a good reason for this twist in terms of aesthetics or construction, and it is hard to believe that the maker would have deliberately made his life difficult by introducing the twist. This feature can be seen on other chairs from the same period, so

it is unlikely that it has been caused by the crest 'unwinding' after it was fitted. Similarly if it appears on other chairs then it is most unlikely that this feature was a problem yet to be ironed out by the maker.

One would have expected that either the crest would have been curved more so that a twist was unnecessary, or the mortices in the seat, arm and crest would have been more closely aligned. Perhaps we will never know the reason?

The Arm-posts

These, like the ribbon slats, are twisted. It is my belief that this twisting occurred after the chair was made and the ends of the arm became bent, most likely because the sapwood on the outside of the arm shrank more than the heartwood that makes up most of the arm.

Twist of ribbon slat.

Shape versus Finish

It has already been observed that the shaping of the components of the chair appears to have been of higher priority to the maker than the cosmetic finish. By today's standards, a judge in a competition would probably eliminate the chair from his consideration purely because of the extensive tool marks left on it. This raises the interesting question of whether a chair with all the tool marks carefully removed would have more, or less merit than the chair under consideration. One thing is certain – it would be much less interesting!

The chair today has a wonderful patina, but it should be realized that these tool marks would have been far more evident when it was freshly made. The turning marks on the spindles, multiple defects in the arm, rough spokeshave marks on the end grain of the seat, and the facets on the cabriole legs would all have stood out to any but the most cursory inspection.

The gap between the hollowing of the seat and the short spindles is ⅛ – ¼in (3–6mm) on the left-hand side, and ½ – ¾in (13–19mm) on the right-hand side; and it has already been noted that the splat is far from symmetrical. These irregularities do not detract from this antique chair, and possibly they enhance it as we can think of them as quaint and typical of the workmanship 250 years ago, smug in the belief that none of the variation would be present in a chair made to modern standards.

My view is that this is to miss the point entirely. I have no doubt that accuracy could have been achieved by the maker, but it was foreign to his way of working, and considered unnecessary. A Windsor made to a great level of accuracy, symmetry and repeatability (for example, the shapes of spindles) is lifeless. Making such a chair by hand is a pointless occupation – far better to leave machines to produce these lifeless chairs inexpensively, and use the skilled hands for something else. The finest Windsors in my opinion are highly organic in nature, with a life of their own.

When I am teaching people to make Windsor chairs it is very hard to get across the completely different approach required, compared with, say, cabinet making, where all must be precise. Tight joints are necessary for the structure to be sound, though Windsors can work for many years with loose joints, but otherwise an accuracy to the nearest ¹⁄₁₆ – ⅛in (2–3mm) is quite sufficient to produce a fine chair. Vernier callipers are not a tool much required by a Windsor chairmaker!

The Philosophy of the Maker

The impression of the maker that I have gained from studying this chair is that he was a highly practical person who worked quickly, confidently, and with an instinctive feel for a pleasing shape. The through-mortice for the splat, with its tapered base, suggests a very practical solution to a particular problem. It suggests someone who was working in his own way, rather than doing things because they had always been done that way.

While studying this chair I was reminded most clearly of a section in George Sturt's *The Wheelwright's Workshop*. This book, first published in 1923, describes his life as a wheelwright near Farnham in Surrey, between 1884 and 1891. In Chapter XVI, entitled 'Tapering and Shaving', he begins with a story about a Farmer Tupp who, when ordering a new wagon, begged the maker not to waste effort, in order to save money, making it beautiful by shaving wood from the timbers in a decorative way. Sturt's response was as follows:

"Truly he was justified (in not wanting decoration for decoration's sake) had this been so. Any farmer might well deprecate such extravagance on his tackle. Usefulness not beauty was wanted… But Farmer Tupp was badly mistaken if he thought that money would be saved by forbidding the wheelwright to spend time in shaving-up the wagon timbers. If indeed by his parsimony he saved a few pounds on his wheelwright's bill, it must eventually have cost him many times as much in horseflesh. For this 'shaving' was one of the ways by which a wheelwright reduced the weight of his always too cumbersome product…"

Sturt next discussed the making of the shafts of a wagon, to which the horse was attached:

"Beginning with three-and-a-half to four inches square near the body, where the shaft had to be very strong, they 'tapered' to three inches at the point. If they didn't, you knew it. To raise from the ground a pair of shafts that had not been duly 'tapered' was to know what the poor horse had been spared.......It happened that properly tapered shafts looked graceful. But I am not aware that this appearance was ever deliberately sought…. He [the wheelwright] felt that it looked right."

He continues in the next paragraph to emphasize the practical nature of the shaping, which I believe accords precisely with the approach required for making the finest Windsor chairs:

"One principle governed all this work… The object was to relieve the horses of every ounce possible. To this end the timbers were pared down, here and there, to a very skeleton thinness. But wherever strength was essential … there nothing was shaved away."

Although Sturt is at pains to stress the utility of this shaving, he acknowledges that the workers took great pride in their work, and I wonder if they did not actually seek to make the waggons attractive, knowing that this achieved the desired result of minimizing weight: 'A man skilful with his draw-shave enjoyed this work, lingering over it like an artist.'

I believe that working to the mental picture of what 'looked right' was probably the only way that a wheelwright could decide when to shave and when to stop.

Conclusion

It may be coincidence that this chair has many similarities to the 'Pitt' chair featured in Chapter 1 *(see page 18)*, and that Pitt was a wheelwright as well as a Windsor chairmaker. However, everything that I have seen in this chair is consistent with Sturt's description of a wheelwright's work. The shaping of the chair is so sure and effective that it must have been done by a person of great skill. The lack of effort made to remove tool marks suggests a person working in a field who does not value the finest detail, but rather the utility and attractiveness of the whole. If the maker of this chair was a wheelwright, I would be not be in the least surprised, though I have no definitive evidence one way or another!

CHAPTER 7

THE BODY LANGUAGE OF CHAIRS, SHAPE AND DESIGN

Body Language

If one is not familiar with a type of furniture, then it is difficult to compare different examples, and to draw any useful conclusions other than perhaps 'one is bigger than the other', or 'one is painted blue and the other red'. Similarly, if designing a chair it is useful to have an appreciation for some of the signals that your chair may send out.

In order for a meaningful comparison to be made, some unifying system for looking at the pieces needs to be found. This might include reference to a small number of 'classic' pieces that are universally considered to define the style/type, so that direct comparisons can be made with a benchmark. Once greater familiarity with the genre is achieved, then the pieces can be deconstructed so that smaller and smaller elements of the furniture can be considered in their own right, compared one to another, and to a benchmark. This approach happens all the time in art, and whole vocabularies, quite unintelligible to the layman, develop. This reinforces a close-knit community, keeps the uninitiated out, and may serve to keep prices high by bamboozling lay collectors!

I would like to propose a simple, and I hope intuitive, approach to looking at, comparing, and thinking about Windsor chairs. This is based on the concept of body language.

Firstly, why should chairs have 'body language'? The answer is that they are designed to support the human body, and therefore in most cases have proportions similar to the human body. Some surfaces are directly in contact with the body, and therefore these surfaces naturally follow its outline. For example the back, seat and front legs outline the shape of a sitting body when viewed from the side; and the arms of a chair generally follow the line of the forearms.

Human beings are very sensitive to non-verbal communication, and some experts believe that 93 per cent of communication is non verbal, made up of 33 per cent vocal tones, and 55 per cent body language. Given that body language makes up such a large proportion of communication it would be surprising if chairs did not have a body language of their own. They cannot speak, so how else can they communicate with us?

We all understand and are sensitive to body language to a greater or lesser extent, and although it can be learned, it is largely innate. This seems to me to give a much more satisfactory and open way of looking at chairs than having to learn a 'vocabulary' that has been invented by experts who have a vested interest in keeping a subject obscure.

So, what messages can a chair send to us?

Superficial Messages

I believe that there are two types of message. First, there are messages that are somewhat superficial, and designed to send messages about the sitter rather than the chair. Such chairs seem to me to be more akin to an extra layer of clothes or decoration for a person.

A good example of this is a throne. I have never seen a Windsor throne (one day...!) but the principle holds good. Thrones always stand out from their surroundings, and are large. Their purpose is to impress, and to enhance the status of the person who is seated. Much intricate and rich decoration may be applied to the surface to show off the wealth, and therefore status, of the sitter. This is like jewellery and clothing that is worn by people of high status, with the intention of impressing others.

This type of message can be found in chairs in all situations.

Think about a dining table and its chairs. It is unusual for all the chairs to be the same: there are usually one or two arm-chairs that are placed at the head of the table. And we all know how much trouble often needs to be taken when a group of people sits down to a meal. One armchair is usually occupied by the host, conveying his higher status in his own home. The other armchair might be occupied by a partner or by an important guest as a gesture of respect. The armchairs are big-ger and more impressive than the armless side chairs, and we are highly tuned to the significance of sitting in them. We may choose to ignore the convention, but this would undoubtedly be an act of conscious or unconscious rebellion against a hier-archy.

The same pattern is seen repeatedly in organizations. The most important person will sit in the largest chair. It may be a matter of size, or the presence of arms that marks out the chair and the person, or it may be a special chair that has been made solely for the leader. This chair is also likely to be somewhat higher that the surrounding chairs to reinforce the dominance of the person.

A Chair's Personality

This is all very well, but is more about human conventions and hierarchies than thinking about the chair itself as an organic object with a personality. This is where I believe Windsor chairs are special in that they so closely follow the human form. Think about the names we give the parts of a Windsor: almost all are parts of the human anatomy – feet, knees, legs, seats, arms, hands, knuckles, backs, ears, and so on.

VARYING THE LEG ANGLES
Let us first consider the simplest of side chairs, from the side. We can see the seat, legs and the back – ignore stretchers and spindles for the time being. By varying the angles of the front and back legs we can completely change the personality of the chair. If the front legs are upright and the back legs angled steeply backwards, we have an energetic-looking chair. The back legs give the appearance of being ready to thrust the chair forwards to meet any challenge.

Change the angle of the front legs so that they are at the same angle as the back legs, but opposite, and the chair

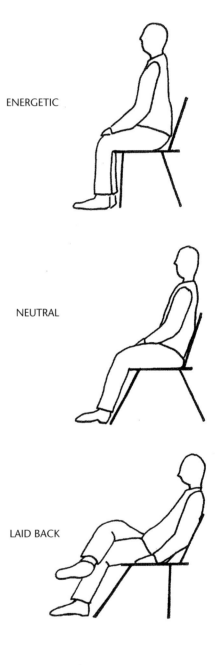

ENERGETIC

NEUTRAL

LAID BACK

The body language of the sitter reflects the body language of the chair.

becomes neutral in appearance. It looks settled, and not expecting to have to move. It is relaxed and sees no threats.

Finally reverse the original arrangement so that the back legs are vertical (not very sensible!) and the front legs stick out to the front. This gives the appearance of a chair that is totally laid back – almost lazy.

Can you picture people in these poses? Some people always look ready for action: they have a vitality about them, which comes in large part form the way they stand – knees slightly bent, and the weight on the balls of their feet. Others just stand as if in a queue, patiently waiting, but knowing that the bus won't arrive for some time yet. Finally there is the youth leaning against the wall, with his hands in his pockets, who couldn't care less what is going on around him.

If you can picture these people, and see how the simple adjustment of leg angles can mimic these human stances, then you will understand how important the choice of angles in a chair is. Be conscious of the messages that you may be sending with your chosen angles, and make sure that the message is appropriate for the situation that your chair will be put in, and its expected use.

For example, if you are making a set of chairs for the boardroom of a dynamic new company, then the last message that you want to send is one of being lazy and not caring what is going on. The thrusting, alert message would be far more appropriate.

Consideration of these body-language messages is not only useful when designing new chairs, it also gives a framework with which to classify existing chairs. It is easy to separate chairs into different styles – for example sack back, comb-back, bow-back – but without a system such as this it is hard to compare them intelligently. We will have our own personal preferences, but they may need to be modified when looking at chairs for different purposes.

ARMS AND ARM-POSTS

Having looked at leg angles, we can take the same skeleton side chair and add arm-posts and an arm. They continue to have the same effect, but there are now more choices to develop the message by adjusting the arm-post angle, and even that of the back.

Take the neutral side chair and add arm posts that are parallel to the back legs. This produces a strong forward-slanting diagonal in the chair that suggests forward movement. Next adjust the arm posts so that they are vertical. This destroys the forward diagonal and gives a more neutral look to the chair. Finally, angle the arm posts back so that they are parallel to the front legs (also possibly the back) and the chair takes on a laid-back personality.

There are so many varied messages that can be given out by just a few small changes. So what else can be done?

THE SPLAY OF THE LEGS

Look at a chair from the front, and a new set of messages can be received. Firstly, the splay of the legs alters the impression of the chair. If the legs are vertical, then the chair appears uptight, as well as being unstable; but the distance between the legs affects the look of stability and solidity. Thus vertical legs with a wide stance look solid, whereas a narrow stance looks weedy. Splayed legs give an air of balance and strength, and work well with the 'thrusting' arrangement seen from the side.

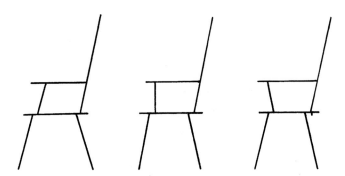

The addition of arms and arm posts can reinforce the effects of the leg arrangement.

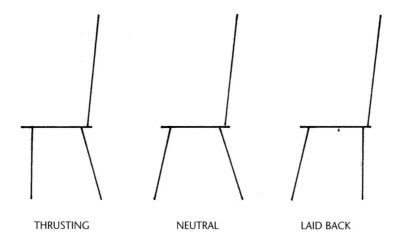

THRUSTING   NEUTRAL   LAID BACK

When viewed from the side the arrangement of the legs affects the character of the chair.

SOLID   THIN   WEEDY   MUSCULAR

Body-forms when viewed from the front.

THE SPINDLES AND BACK

The arrangement of the spindles and the back itself adds to the messages from the legs. A narrow parallel-sided back on narrow legs gives the impression of thinness, but not necessarily weakness. However, taper the back so that the top is narrower than the base, and you have a chair with narrow shoulders – a definite sign of weakness. Conversely, splay the back to give broad shoulders, and you have a strong muscular chair, whether or not it is heavy or lightweight; in a person it could be considered athletic. With splayed legs we have broad shoulders, a narrow waist and a broad stance – an 'ideal' male profile.

If the chair is broad, and with little splay in the legs and the back, it suggests a very solid person and personality. It can appear to be strong as well, but definitely not light on its feet.

THE ARMS

The arms are also used in conveying messages. If you greet a long-lost friend, you are likely to extend your arms to them with your hands wide apart in welcome. Chairs with arms that diverge towards the front are much more welcoming than those with arms that are parallel. Parallel arms in a greeting say, 'Welcome, but I don't want to hug you!'

The least welcoming arm message is to keep them wrapped around your body protectively. This definitely discourages close contact with another person, but makes the owner of the arms feel secure. Similarly a chair with arms that wrap around the sitter slightly – they cannot wrap around too much or there would be no room to sit down – give a feeling of security to the sitter, but do not welcome anyone to sit down.

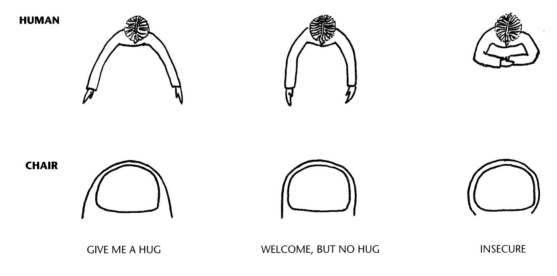

HUMAN

CHAIR

GIVE ME A HUG   WELCOME, BUT NO HUG   INSECURE

Does the chair welcome the sitter?

FRONT   **SIDE**

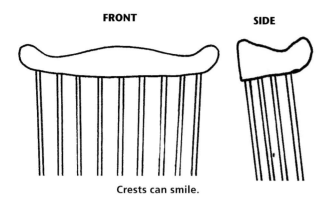

Crests can smile.

THE SHAPE OF THE CREST

Finally, a chair with a crest can convey emotions. Car makers for some time have given considerable attention to the front of cars to ensure they don't give the wrong signals. It is easy enough to make the radiator grill of a car point down at the ends, giving a decidedly grumpy or sad expression, if you consider it as a mouth. Similarly crests can be upward or downward pointing, depending on the shape and orientation.

A crest with a straight bottom, but which is mounted perpendicular to spindles that slope backwards, will appear to curve upwards like a smile when seen from the front; furthermore the uplift will be enhanced with greater angles to the spindles, and also as the crest is curved more towards the front of the chair.

The shape of the crest other than the base also makes a difference. If it has ears that lift at the ends, as is traditional in many American chairs, then this will add to the 'smile'; they might also be considered to be like dimples on either side of a mouth. If, however, the ears point downwards, as is found in some Victorian English chairs, then however much the base gives an uplift, the overall impression will be gloomy.

The Anatomy of Windsor Chairs

As a maker I have over the years developed my own ideas about what makes for a good Windsor chair. I am not trained in art or design but I have made many chairs, including designs of my own, and have drawn a number of conclusions about what is visually satisfying and what is not. None of these should be considered definitive, but the following ideas and range of dimensions may help to provide some guidelines when designing a new chair or modifying an old design.

Overall Scale

The proportions of a chair are largely determined by its function of supporting a human frame. It seems to be the current convention to make the top of the front of the seat 18in (45cm) above the ground. For a chair in isolation, a variation of height +/–½in (13mm) up to +/–1in (25mm) still works satisfactorily for people of widely different heights. However, if the chair is for sitting up to a table to work or eat, then the chosen height will only be ideal for a limited number of people. Fortunately humans are very adaptable, but the height of the seat above the ground is one of the most fundamental parameters in designing a chair.

The dimensions of the seat come from the size and shape of the human bottom, and whether the chair has arms or not. The width of the seat is normally wider than the depth. The widths of most chairs fall into the range 17–24in (43–60cm), with the smaller dimensions suitable for side chairs (those without arms).

The depth of the seat would normally range from 16–19in (40–48cm). Some people with long legs like a very deep seat to give support under their thighs, but a well shaped stool seat of 12in (30cm) diameter can be very comfortable, and extreme depths would only be made to fulfil a specific request.

The height of the back can vary enormously, and many different heights are comfortable. This book has been written sitting on a chair with a 13in (33cm) high back, but chairs with a 30in (45cm) back can be equally comfortable. More important than height is the shape and angle of the back.

The arms of a chair are normally 8–10in (20–25cm) above the seat.

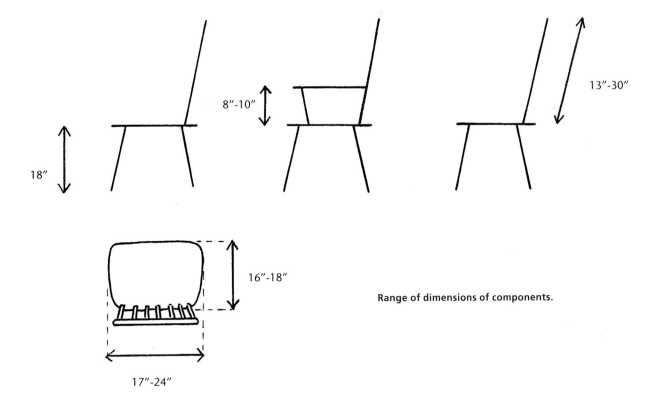

8"-10"

13"-30"

18"

16"-18"

17"-24"

Range of dimensions of components.

All these measurements are derived from the range of measurements and the proportions of the human frame; but as already mentioned we are very adaptable, and can be comfortable on a wide range of chairs of differing shapes and sizes.

The Seat

Almost all Windsor chairs have a seat between 1⅜in (3.5cm) and 2in (5cm) thick. When made of a hard wood such as elm, this can lead to a very heavy chair. All the finest chairs have had a large proportion of their mass removed in order to make them more comfortable and to reduce weight. However, we tend to judge chairs more by eye than feel, and so merely removing wood to reduce weight may not be sufficient to make a great chair. If the eye does not immediately judge that the seat has been significantly lightened, then, however much wood has actually been removed, the chair will still be considered heavy. Thus the way in which wood is removed is very important, and every trick should be used to fool the eye into believing that more wood has been removed than may actually be the case.

As an example when making a sack-back seat in elm, the weight was recorded at different stages (*see* table on page 150).

Almost half of the weight loss came from shaping, smoothing and chamfering after the adzing. The visual effect of the latter processes is far greater than the original adzing, but with slightly less weight loss.

Chamfering

Chamfering is a skill that must be learned in order to make a successful chair. The word 'chamfer' comes from two words: 'edge' and 'break', and 'breaking edges' can have a very positive effect on furniture, for very little effort.

Chamfers do not have to be sophisticated to work; for example, a rough chamfer on the bottom edge of the seat can reduce the apparent thickness by ¼in (6mm) for a couple of minutes' work. Think how much effort would be required to remove ¼in thickness from a whole seat!

	Weight after process (kg)	Weight loss (kg)	% of original weight lost by this process
Elm seat blank 1¾in (4.4cm) thick	5.20	0	0
Adzing	4.38	0.82	16
Shaping, smoothing and chamfering	3.58	0.80	15
Total weight loss	1.62	1.62	31

In fact chairmakers of old never wasted effort or materials, because their livelihood depended on minimizing their input. Look at the legs on old chairs and see how often there are 'flat spots' where insufficient wood was used to obtain a complete cylinder. With seats they used sufficiently thick wood to produce the degree of hollowing that they desired. However, in almost every case the looks of the chair were improved by chamfering the seat.

The principle that 'less is more' applies as much to seats as to any other part of the chair. Few chairs of distinction have any more wood left in them than is absolutely necessary, and this search to remove wood may be the origin of the unique shape of the American 'shield' seat. The hollows on each side, shaped somewhat like a violin, add considerably to the effort required to make the seat, so they must have had a purpose originally. I believe that they were developed because there was no need for wood in this location and so it was removed. The attractive result has caused this feature to survive.

Having discussed methods to lighten a seat, it is conversely important that it should look strong enough in key places. The shield seat is again an excellent example of this. The eye needs to see a substantial thickness of wood where the bow and spindles enter the seat, whereas elsewhere such reassurance is not required and can be avoided, depending on the design.

When shaping a seat nothing spoils the desired effect more than transitions between surfaces that are not crisp. It is very easy to allow the hollow part of the seat to merge into the platform at the back so that no one knows precisely where one finishes and the other begins. If care is taken with hollowing tools and abrasives to produce a crisp line of transition, the resulting chair will benefit. American chairs often have this particular transition emphasized by the presence of the 'rain gutter' – a carved 'U'-shaped line that marks the change of shape. This feature is not found on English chairs, but a variety of edge treatments were undertaken, which draw the eye away from the thickness of the seat.

Crisp detail is also important over the rest of the seat, whether it is the sharp edge of an American bow-back chair between the top surface and the chamfer underneath, or the shaping of the front of an English chair where there may be a chamfer at the bottom with a vertical section before the top surface. Nobody would like a chair with sharp edges, but a line that has been made crisp initially and subsequently softened with abrasives will always be preferable to an edge that has been carelessly made and has no definition.

Through-tenons with contrasting wedges add to the visual interest of a chair, and provide an immediate understanding to the viewer of the method of construction.

The 'nose' of a seat and the front edge are probably the most variable aspects of Windsor seating, and they offer the maker a chance to express his personal preferences. Some noses rise to a point, others are gently curved, and some chairs have no evidence of where the centre of the seat lies, because the front edge is horizontal. If one considers the bow-back chair, the effect of raising or lowering the front edge can make a dramatic effect on the chair's appearance. The maker will develop a preference that may change over time – or at a whim!

The Chair Legs

The legs of a chair have the fundamental task of supporting the weight of the sitter so that the chair doesn't break and the sitter doesn't fall off. Leaving aside the myriad patterns of turning on both sides of the Atlantic, we should consider first the arrangement of the legs in the seat.

The back of a chair tends to constrain the bottom of the sitter to within a small area. However, as the sitter moves around in the chair – whether sitting upright, slouching or turning to one side – the bottom remains close to the intended spot close to the centre line. For this reason the back legs do not need to be especially far apart, and on almost all chairs the distance between the feet of the back legs is less than that of the front legs.

A wider stance of the front legs is necessary to prevent the chair tipping over when the sitter rotates in the seat or puts pressure on one side when rising or sitting. The width of the stance is different from the splay of legs – the angle from the vertical when viewed from the front – and the reduction in width of stance from front to back can be achieved in a number of different ways by varying the splay.

The front legs of American chairs tend to have greater splay than those of their English cousins, and structural reasons for this have been discussed elsewhere. However, it should be noted that it is quite possible for the splay of the front legs to be less than that of the rear legs, and yet for the width of stance to be greater.

Fundamental Patterns

THE ARMS

The arms of Windsor chairs are either steam-bent or 'sawn' (built up of three or more pieces of flat wood jointed together and shaped). The back of the arm tends to follow the shape of the back of the seat, but then deviates as it moves forwards. This arrangement allows spindles to be spaced evenly, and if they pass through the arm, to be able to fit into a bow or crest which will also tend to follow a similar curve.

It is traditional in American chairs for the arm to tilt backwards over the seat, in the same way that the seat tilts backwards over the floor. Aesthetically, this avoids having the seat surface and arm as two parallel planes, which can detract from the organic nature of these chairs. Just as there are few right-angles and flat surfaces, so there are very few instances of planes or lines being parallel. Even if spindles are evenly spaced with no splay, their own shape, which varies over their length, partially disguises the parallel nature of their axes.

Some old English arms are tilted in the opposite direction. In others the bottom of the arm may be parallel to the seat, but the top surface of the arm is tapered towards the front, again disguising the parallel nature.

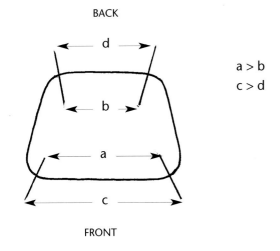

BACK

$a > b$
$c > d$

FRONT

Front legs vs. back legs.

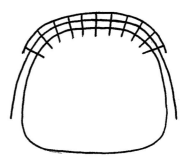

**The arm and crest of a chair
follow the back of the seat
around the centre line.**

151

It is possible to vary the cross-section of arms considerably along their length. This can have the effect of minimizing the visual and physical weight of the arm, and is particularly relevant in heavy arms.

THE BOW

English arms and bows are often more rectangular in shape than their American counterparts, with much tighter radii at the 'shoulders', whereas the curvature of American bends tends to be smoother. American bows tend to be based on a circle, while English bows rely on a more oval profile. The oval top means that the tightest radius is at the shoulders of an English bow.

The cross-section of bows was another part of the chair where individual preference could be expressed. Bows vary from square, to rectangular, to round, to square with a quarter-round and finally one flat face and the remainder rounded. The thickness of English bows was frequently disguised by adding one or two grooves to a flat surface.

One final feature that I have seen only on English chairs is the bow that has a flat front and inner face with the front face twisted in towards the centre. This attractive effect can be achieved by rounding over the back edge of the bow prior to steam-bending. As the bow is bent it twists inwards because the cross-section is not symmetrical.

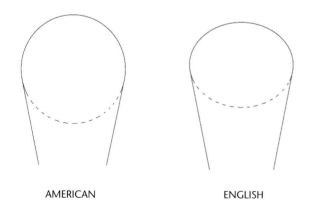

AMERICAN   ENGLISH

American bows tend to be circular, while English bows often have 'shoulders'.

The part of the bow that most often lets the chair down is just before the bow enters the seat or the arm. Usually a round tenon is formed either by hand or with a tenon cutter, and particularly with the latter a shoulder will be formed. Unless care is taken to lose that shoulder and smooth the transition from round tenon to, for example, a square bow with rounded corners, the discontinuity of shape will attract the eye and spoil the chair.

Makers in the past have developed many different strategies for this part of the bow. Sometimes a round tenon is formed with a very sudden shoulder, and the square section of the bow is let into the seat hiding the shoulder entirely. Frequently makers of the early English double-bow chairs formed a rectangular tenon at the ends of the bows, which was roughly parallel to the curve of the arm. The front face of the bow was then shaped also to align with the arm, and this necessitated careful shaping of the other faces to prevent any discontinuities.

THE CONTINUOUS BOW

The most complex shape of bow that was successful was the continuous bow or continuous arm. This American development from around 1790 was perfected in the New York area and involved bending the bow in two planes. The process is not as complex as it might appear once a suitable former has been made. The back of the bow is bent around a former often very close to semi-circular. This is held on a horizontal surface and the arms are then bent in a separate operation while the wood retains it heat and plasticity.

It is unusual for the bow to be of constant cross-section along its whole length. As with some English arms, the thickness was normally reduced where the arm was bent for the second time to make the arms of the bow. The thickness was then either kept constant to the hands, or increased after the bend.

One of the greatest challenges of this bend is keeping the bent wood in the correct shape while it dries. If there is only one bend, then it can be left in the former for days while the moisture level drops. Normally, however, more than one is bent at a time in order to spread the effort required to set up the steaming equipment and the fuel used to set the water boiling over as many bends as possible. Also the bending equipment is often located outside or in an unheated shed, and the drying will be very slow and incomplete.

It is worth making simple 'keeps' for the bent bows, which keep the main bend in place with the arms a constant width apart, and a string to apply tension to the top bow to maintain the second bend until it dries. There is little time available between releasing the newly bent wood from the former and fitting it to the keep if the bends are not to unwind, and a second pair of hands can be invaluable at this stage. The radius of the bends will tend to increase during this move from former to keep, and considerable pressure will be necessary to re-establish the original angle between back and arms, which will be maintained by the string while drying.

It should be noted that it is not necessary, or desirable, to bend the arms perpendicular to the back. An angle of 110 to 115 degrees works well, and produces an elegant shape. This reduced angle of bend makes the bending easier, and is likely to be more successful. A right-angle would lead to a very flat back, which would be neither strong, comfortable nor elegant.

The continuous bow from the 1790s is bent in two planes, but there is no reason why an arm should not be bent in continuously varying planes. A more complex and three-dimensional former can be built, and this offers a wide range of interesting new possibilities for design.

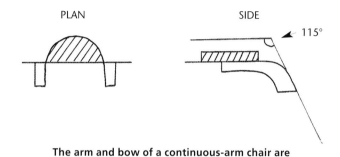

PLAN SIDE

115°

The arm and bow of a continuous-arm chair are not at 90 degrees.

Windsor continuous arm settee with bending former in the foreground. Note the continuous bend, compared with the traditional former that only bends in two planes.

THE ARM-POSTS

American armchairs always had turned arm-posts, and the pattern of turning would be in the same style as the legs, stretchers and back-posts (if present). However, the early English chairs had two variations on the turned post (which became the norm in the nineteenth century). Some of the earliest English armchairs had flat arm-posts, which may or may not have been pierced; these were secured to the seat and the arm with round tenons, and often inserted vertically into the seat (*see* Chapter 8).

The most common variety in the latter half of the seventeenth century were steam-bent arm-posts, usually made of the same wood as the arm. These posts tended to be straight from just above the seat to the bottom of the tenon, and then to curve through approximately 45 degrees up to the arm. They were secured to the arm with screws, nails or dowels. They were from ¾–1in (19–25mm) in diameter.

THE CREST

Most crests are curved, but there are a number of examples of straight crests, particularly on settees; however, these are a special case of the general principle that crests tend to follow the curve of the back of the seat and the arm, if present. The straight crests tend to be relatively short, following the straight back of a settee, but ending before the arm and seat curve round to the front. This principle rarely applies perfectly, as the curve of the crest often reduces towards each end, just as the arm and seat continue to curve forwards, but it acts as a good guide when designing a new chair.

The crest is designed to move mainly backwards and forwards when pressure is applied to the back, although a twisting motion will be applied when the sitter leans to one side. In order for the back to remain intact it is important that joints in the crest remain close to neutral in terms of compression and tension. If the spindles all appear parallel when viewed from the side, then neutrality will be maintained when the crest moves forwards and back, even if they are splayed when viewed from the front.

Problems can arise when spindles are not parallel when viewed from the side. This arrangement gives a back that cannot flex, because of the triangulation caused by the spindles. If the chair is deliberately designed this way, and the spindles are secured at each end and the centre, then a strong and stiff

If the spindles in a crest are parallel when viewed from the side then the back can flex front to back. If they are splayed then triangulation prevents front to back movement.

back will ensue; however, this would be an unusual arrangement for a Windsor, and a thicker crest than normal would be required to be able to drill the mortices at many different angles. This triangulation should normally be avoided, as backward pressure on the crest will tend to put the central joints into compression, and the outer joints into tension. If, as is usual, only three tenons are pinned (the central one, and the two outer) then enormous pressure will be put on the outer pins, and the integrity of the whole back will depend on their strength alone.

Crests have many different shapes, but frequently the ends are shaped as ears, in both English and American chairs. These rounded ends may be left plain, or carved in spiral patterns (American). Between the ears American crests are simple, rising towards the centre, but the English tradition often involved more complex shaping, including the removal of wood with a fretsaw. This had the effect of adding decoration and at the same time lightening an otherwise heavy crest.

It is tempting sometimes to place the outer spindles very close to the ends of the crest, for the sake of appearance. If this is done then it is vital that the fit is not too tight, and that there is no twist applied to the spindle, causing the wood at the end of the crest to split.

The final consideration in shaping crests is the shape of the cross-section. Sufficient wood needs to be present around the spindle mortices, but as one rises above this point, strength becomes less important and the wood can taper. Many permutations are possible: vertical front face, tapered back; tapered front face, vertical back; tapered on both sides; parallel on both sides, rounded and tapered at the top; and so on. English crests tend to be much heavier than American as they may support thicker spindles, slats and splats, and they need to be in proportion.

THE SPINDLES

The 'standard' angle for a side chair is around 12 to 14 degrees, and this would be a good angle to start with if designing a new side chair. Assuming the side chair is to be used up to a table, the angle might vary from 10 to 14 degrees: any less, and the sitter will feel that the back is forcing him forwards into an unnatural position; any more, and the sitter will feel laid back and unable to 'sit up' attentively. The 'ideal' angle is purely a matter of personal preference, but the range of 10 to 14 degrees would suit most people.

An armchair used as a carver at a dining table would tend to be slightly more laid back, with a suitable range of perhaps 11 to 15 degrees; but if it is to be used on its own for reading and relaxing, then a range of 13 to 18 degrees would be more appropriate.

RANGE OF ANGLES

Legs: The angle for Windsor legs varies from, say, 5 to 28 degrees. The front legs of English chairs will commonly have an angle of less than 10 degrees, while those of American chairs are in the range of 10 to 20 degrees. The back legs of English chairs may range from 12 to 25 degrees, and of American chairs from 15 to 28 degrees. These angles refer to the angle from the vertical along the sight-line, which will generate a combination of rake and splay depending on the direction of the sight-line.

Arm-posts: These range from vertical to 25 degrees on American chairs, and vertical to 20 degrees on English chairs. The curved steam-bent arm-posts were inserted either vertically, or at an angle up to 15 degrees.

Back-posts: These mirrored the angles of spindles in the back, and therefore range from 10 to 20 degrees, depending on the style of chair and its intended purpose.

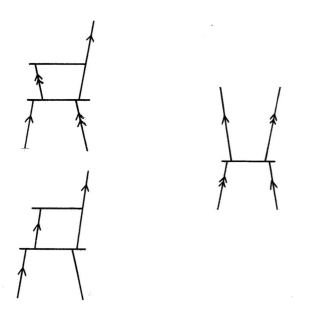

Arranging components so that they appear parallel from the front or side can be visually satisfactory.

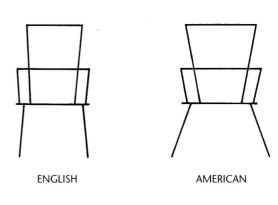

ENGLISH   AMERICAN

By simply adjusting the splay of components one can create either an American or English profile.

MATCHING ANGLES

If you design a chair from scratch then the range of angles described above gives an infinite number of combinations, and this may be overwhelming. However, to simplify matters it may be worth matching the angles of different parts. For example, you may arrive at an attractive combination of angles and sight-lines for the legs of a new chair, and then wonder what to do about the arm-posts and back-posts.

Looking from the side of the chair, you might decide to match the angle of the arm-post to the back legs, so that the chair has a strong diagonal in its design running from the bottom of the back leg through the seat to the top of the arm-post. If the front leg is not heavily raked to the front, then the arm-post could be matched to the front leg so that it is angled slightly backwards – see the section 'Body Language' on pages 144 to 147. Similarly the back-posts can be angled so that they are parallel to the front legs.

This approach can also be used when looking at the chair from the front, although the matching angle would be between arm-post/ back-post and the front/ back legs on the opposite side. The effect of this matching is to give an 'X' pattern to the front view of the chair if the elements are well splayed, as in many American chairs. By matching angles from the front, and adjusting them, one can easily produce the outlines of 'English' and 'American' chairs.

Try out different combinations either by drawing or model making before drilling holes in a seat. The time spent doing this will save both time and resources in the longer term. Models can be made from expanded polystyrene for seats and wire pushed into the seats for turnings and spindles.

Rocking Chairs

These are something of a special case, and the angle of the spindles in a rocker designed purely for relaxation may reach 20 degrees. If this is combined with a seat that sits at a considerable angle to the floor, then a much larger proportion of the sitter's weight is taken on the spindles than in a normal chair. This spreads the weight over an even greater area, enhancing the overall comfort.

The angles of the legs will need to be decided on both aesthetically and with consideration for the position of the centre of gravity of the sitter relative to the bottom of the legs. The ranges given above will remain generally appropriate, but the positions of the tenons may need to be adjusted.

The greatest consideration concerning rocker legs is that the front and back legs should lie in the same plane when looked at from the front. This means that the feet and the tenons in the seat must form a single plane, which may be splayed as much or as little as desired. If the rocker and legs are in the same plane, then the rocker will lie parallel to the tenons of the legs in the seat. This is a useful tip when designing a rocker from scratch. It would be unusual in a Windsor for the leg tenons to be equidistant from the centre-line of the seat, but if they were, then the rockers would be parallel. Visually this would not be ideal, as the rockers might then appear to be wider apart at the back than at the front – quite the opposite of what one would expect, and therefore visually unsettling. Conversely if the back leg tenons are much closer together than the front legs, then the rockers will converge as one moves to the back of the chair, and in extreme cases, or

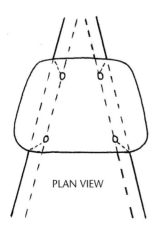

The rockers will be parallel to a line between the tenons in the seat.

The centre of gravity of the combined chair and sitter must not be allowed to move behind the back of the rockers.

with extra long rockers, they might even cross – which would be difficult to build!

The centre of gravity of the combined sitter and chair must never be allowed to come close to the back of the rockers. If it does, then an extra-vigorous rock by the sitter will send him past the point of balance and on to his back. This can be avoided by adjusting the following: the length of the rockers; the angle of the back legs; the radius of the rockers; and the height of the seat over the ground.

Designing Your Own Chair

Where does one start? Designing a chair can be a daunting prospect if you do not have a systematic way of approaching it, and this is what this section will attempt to provide.

One could randomly select measurements and angles, and hope for the best, but the chances of producing an attractive chair are remote. It is far easier, and more productive, to find a chair that you like and use information from it as a starting point for your chair. You may not have access to the actual chair, but a photograph can provide a wealth of information if studied carefully. If you are lucky a photo will be accompanied by some basic measurements; but if not, it may be possible to estimate sizes by assuming that the height of the seat is 18in (45cm), and scaling other components by measuring. Even a photo taken from an angle with distortion due to perspective can be useful, and at least the dimensions gained will be close to the original.

It is very unusual to achieve an ideal chair on the first attempt. It is more likely that you will make the first chair, and after considering it for some time, make a second with a number of changes, large and small. A third chair is frequently needed to produce a shape that you are really satisfied with, and even that may be improved by small changes with each repetition.

In the early years of my chairmaking I tended to develop a new chair by making incremental changes to existing chairs that I had made. I soon realized that this was an unnecessarily labour-intensive process, where each prototype had to be completed before beginning to improve the next version.
I concluded that making changes to a design on paper was much less effort than making a whole new chair. It required spending several hours in the planning/drawing stage rather than making shavings in the workshop, but the cost of paper and pencil is much less than wasting a full set of materials and many more hours on a chair.

In fact this design process can be one of the most satisfying aspects of Windsor chairmaking. To take an idea from one's head and convert it into a three-dimensional object is a great achievement, and of another order compared with following a pre-existing plan. There is a place for using plans when starting out and developing one's making skills, but I would urge anyone to aim to make their own-design chairs eventually.

If it looks good on paper it will look good in wood. Perhaps this is stating the obvious, but it still surprises me when it works!

Drawing a Chair

Rectilinear furniture is relatively easy to draw, by adopting three views: front, side and top (plan). Windsor furniture offers significant challenges because there are no straight lines, and nothing is at right-angles. However, with careful thought the same three-view system can be made to work.

Most of my chairs start with an idea about one small feature, and develop from there. It might be the shape of a bow, seat, crest, arm, legs …Or I might be doodling and arrive at a pleasant shape that deserves exploring further. Frequently I will sketch a chair in pencil the size of a postage stamp.

Sometimes I attempt perspective, but usually I settle for one of the standard (front, side, top) views. If I like the little sketch I will make more, and start to think about the other views before attempting to draw to scale. If these tiny sketches look good then I have the basis for a new chair, and I have often scaled up one of these tiny sketches to produce a new chair. Once you have the chairmaking bug, you will learn to fill odd moments doodling, developing your ideas about what shapes you like, and hopefully arriving at an inspiration that you can turn into a real chair.

MAKING A START
Whatever your starting point, whether it is an existing chair or a tiny doodle, you will probably have one view that you like best. Take this as your starting point for producing a scale drawing.

Graph paper is ideal for this job, although not too fine a

scale; and squared paper may work for you just as well. You will soon find the type of paper that best suits your way of working. Decide on your scale and set to work adding the basic information that you have to the paper.

If you are drawing the top or front views, which are symmetrical about the centre line, then concentrate on just one half of the chair. When you are happy with the half, it is easy to sketch in the opposite half to get an idea of the whole. This way you only need to make one set of changes each time you alter something – a great saving in time and effort.

In all your drawings I recommend that you base them around the seat. The seat is a plane (although it may be heavily shaped), but keep this plane horizontal to the grid lines on your paper. This way, your seat will be horizontal when viewed from the side, and the floor will probably be drawn at an angle, as the front of the seat is usually higher than the back over the floor.

Similarly when viewed from the front you will only see the thickness of the seat, but the feet of the legs are likely to be at different heights, giving the impression of a sloping floor. Using this system, the outline view of the seat will be geometrically similar to the template that you will later use to cut out the seat. Other parts will be distorted to a greater or lesser extent, but the seat will be accurate. In practice I have found that the levels of distortion can be lived with.

At this stage you will need to decide on a number of starting measurements. These may come from an existing chair, by scaling up from a tiny sketch or a photograph, or they may relate to a constraint in the environment in which the chair will eventually be used (for example, the height of the arm so that it will fit under a particular table). The more measurements you start with, the easier the initial drawing will be, but you may decide to work many of them out as you go along by deciding what looks right in the drawing.

THE FRONT VIEW

Let us assume that you start with the front view. Draw in the vertical centre line and the thickness of the seat on one side only. Mark on the width of the seat. If you know the height of the top of the seat above the ground at the front, usually 18in (45cm), then you can draw a line representing the floor at the front legs. Similarly you can do the same for the back legs, often ½–¾in (13–19mm) less.

You now have the opportunity to draw in the front and back legs and decide on an appropriate splay – that is, angle to the side. The top of the legs cannot enter the seat anywhere, but the splay will be determined by the style of seat that you choose. For example, if you choose an American-style seat, the point of insertion will be well in from the side with a larger splay, whereas in an English seat the insertion will be closer to the edge with a lesser splay. Don't worry too much at this stage over the precise point, as it can be modified as you develop the other two views. Most importantly arrange the legs so

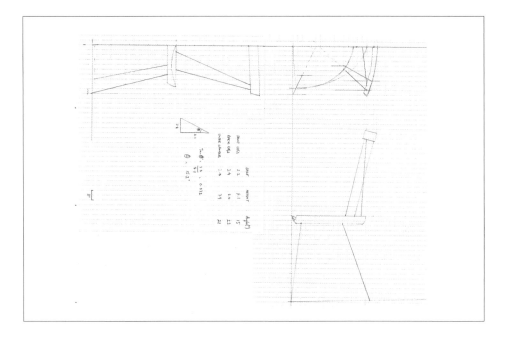

Chairs can be drawn simply on squared paper using front, side and plan elevations, but keeping the seat horizontal in front and side views.

that they look right to you when viewed from the front.

Next you will have to consider the superstructure of your chair. If it has arms, then decide on an appropriate height above the seat, and the splay (if any) of the arm-posts. Draw them in, and adjust them until they look right. If the arm is steam-bent as in a double bow, then continue the line around the back of the chair, but do not forget to take account of the fact that the back of the arm may be lower than the front. Mark in the maximum height of the back, and consider the splay of spindles and any back-posts. The maximum width of a chair is usually at the hands.

THE PLAN AND SIDE VIEWS

With the front view settled (for the moment), prepare a plan view. The width of the seat and splay of the legs should be projected from the front view. Draw out the profile of the seat.

At this stage it may be helpful to begin the side view. The length of the seat can be projected at right-angles to the plan view, and its thickness and shape drawn also. Draw in the ground, which will slope up towards the back. Now the legs can be drawn in, and the position of the tops and bottoms can be settled. When this has been done, the legs can be marked on to the plan view using the information from the other two views. The direction of a leg seen in plan view is the sight-line for drilling, and by projecting the lines across the seat all the information will be available for marking up the seat ready for drilling.

As with the legs, other components can be marked on to one view and then projected on to the other. A process of adjustment backwards and forwards between the views will probably be necessary to produce a satisfactory design.

Most measurements can be taken direct from the plans, but a further step is required to find the angles. Trigonometry will do the job, but it is far simpler to draw a right-angled triangle to scale with the height and base measurements taken from your plan. Measure the angle between the height and hypotenuse with a protractor. This can be used for legs, arm-posts, back-posts and spindles, though I personally do not recommend using it for most spindles – it can be useful for calculating the angle of the central spindle, but use the 'aiming' method for drilling most spindle holes as much as possible, because it is much simpler and adapts to the small variations that occur in each chair.

With all the information gleaned from the plan, a seat template must be created, and in this, modern technology can be a great help. Scan the plan view into a computer and crop the image tight to the centre line and either end of the seat. Set the page size in a desktop publishing programme such as Microsoft Publisher, or a Vector drawing programme such as Corel Draw to be, say, 2in (5cm) larger that the final size of the seat in width and length.

Transfer the image on to the page, and expand it to the desired size (which will leave a 1in (2.5cm) margin all around the page). Then print the document. Unless the seat is very small, it will print on several sheets of paper; but these can be taped together to give the full-size shape. Cut around the shape and use it to mark out your seat on your seat blank. This process of enlarging from a scale drawing to full size can be used for many components, including bending forms for bows and crests.

With a little practice these drawing techniques become very easy, and chairmakers should always be playing around with new ideas for the future. The investment required to produce a new design in this way is far less than that required to build a prototype in wood from scratch.

A more modern method of designing chairs is to use computer-aided design (CAD) programmes such as SketchUP; and much useful information in available on the internet. If you are prepared to take the time to learn how to use these programmes then you will be in the great position of being able to view your designs through 360 degrees. I wish you luck!

CHAPTER 8

WINDSOR FURNITURE OTHER THAN CHAIRS

Windsor furniture is not restricted to just chairs. This very brief chapter includes a few non-standard chairs, and gives a glimpse of other items of furniture that can be made using Windsor construction methods.

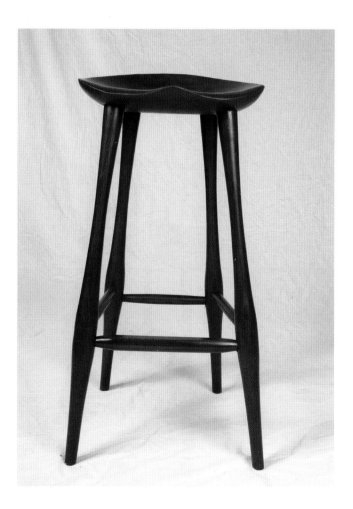

Seating

Stools
The photographs show a simple four-legged stool in oak with bamboo-style legs and a turned top, and a painted high stool

Piano stool.

with a seat carved from 3in thick stock with legs let into the bottom of the seat and through tenoned.

Piano Stool

Up to three players can sit on this bench, made from English oak and elm. The deeply-shaped seat encourages a good posture in the player.

High Chair

English oak and elm, painted with milk paint and finished with linseed oil. A painted high stool with a seat carved from 3in-(7.5cm-) thick stock with legs let into the bottom of the seat and through-tenoned. This design is based on American high chairs from around 1750.

High chair.

Rocking chair.

Rocking Chair

This is a very large chair! The arms are not connected to the back posts and 'float' above the seat. The back is braced with two extra spindles, which are socketed into a tail piece projecting behind the seat. Structurally they are not essential. The back legs are tenoned into the seat behind the spindles, and the legs are joined together by elm rockers that have been sawn from a plank following the curved grain as much as possible. The short back legs, and longer front legs, hold the seat at a considerable angle to the ground. Combining this seat orientation with the central spindle at almost 20 degrees from the vertical, the sitter lays back in a relaxing posture with his weight spread between the spindles and the back.

Conversation Piece

English oak and elm. Two chairs in one with a small 'table' between them. The two chairs are angled towards each other to encourage conversation. The arms 'float' – that is, they are not attached to the backs – and this allows the nine-spindled back to flex with the movements of the sitter. The single piece of elm for the seat was shaped in the usual way, with the exception of the 'table' which was routed.

Conversation Piece.

Wine table.

Tables

Wine Table

Ash stem, American cherry top and base. The simplest possible Windsor table is probably a candle stand, or wine table. A turned stem is socketed into the solid, turned or carved base, and a small table top is secured to the top. In this case a turned collar sits over the tenon at the top of the stem, and the table top is attached to the collar with two screws.

Candle Stand

American cherry. This tripod table is a delightfully delicate piece. The long legs require careful turning to avoid vibration, and the stretchers are not in a single plane as the legs do not have enough depth to accept two tenons at the same height. The legs are tenoned through the top.

Candle stand.

Circular dining table.

Circular Dining Table

English and European oak. The circular dining table has a 5ft (1.5m) diameter top and is made entirely of oak. The spindles, which are socketed into the base, are arranged in six pairs. Each pair is made of one longer and one shorter spindle, and they come together under the top and are tenoned into a block. The six blocks are screwed to the top to secure it. With the flexibility in the spindles there is no need to allow for expansion and contraction of the top due to changes in moisture. With the top secured to six blocks and with enormous triangulation from the pairs of spindles, the top is very firmly held. This feature, along with the low centre of gravity, makes the table much more stable than most circular tables. The arrangement of spindles has the other advantage of not interfering with the legs of anybody sitting up to the table.

Trestle Table

English oak. This table does not have the solid plank base of other Windsor furniture, but the principles are still the same. Triangulation of the spindles gives a rigid support for the top with the minimum of mass. This 'airy' structure is reminiscent of the American Windsor chairs, and has the benefit of not interfering with sitters' legs.

Trestle table.

165

Racks

Towel Rack

Elm and English oak. This towel rack has a solid elm base into which the four main supporting spindles are socketed. Unlike traditional racks this is very stable due to its low centre of gravity. Triangulation of the spindles gives a stiff but light structure.

Cradles

Cradle

Windsor cradles fit into the Windsor definition perfectly. A great variety of designs were made. The spindles were held together either by steam-bent wood or by turned pieces, such as in this illustration.

Towel rack.

Windsor cradle (Courtesy Charles Santore).

FURTHER READING

Alexander, John D. Jr *Make a Chair from a Tree* (Fine Woodworking, 1978) Classic book on green woodworking techniques

Arnold, James *The Shell Book of Country Crafts* (John Baker, 1968) Chapters on country crafts including one on Windsor chairmaking

Blanchard, Roberta Ray *How to Restore and Decorate Chairs* (Avenel, 1952) Details of techniques and patterns for painting and decorating chairs, including Windsors

Cotton, Bernard D. *The English Regional Chair* (Antique Collector's Club, 1990) The definitive book on country chairs, with a large section on Windsors

Crispin, Thomas *The English Windsor Chair* (Alan Sutton, 1992) A historical overview of Windsor chairs

Dunbar, Michael *Make a Windsor Chair* (The Taunton Press, 1984) An excellent practical book on making American-style Windsors

Edwards, Ralph *English Chairs* (HMSO, 1951) Review of chairs in the Victoria & Albert Museum

Gloag, John *The Englishman's Chair* (Allen & Unwin, 1964)

Goyne Evans, Nancy *American Windsor Chairs* (Hudson Hills Press, 1996) The definitive book on American Windsors

Goyne Evans, Nancy *American Windsor Furniture* (Hudson Hills Press, 1997) Covers Windsor furniture in the widest sense – mainly American

Goyne Evans, Nancy *Windsor Chairmaking in America* (UPNE, 2006) Details of working practices, workshops, methods of making and painting, marketing and distribution

Harding-Hill, Michael *Windsor Chairs* (Antique Collector's Club, 2003) Beautiful pictures concentrating on eighteenth-century English Windsors with a section on the nineteenth century

Kassay, John *The Book of American Windsor Furniture* (University of Massachusetts Press, 1998) Photographs and measured drawings of American chairs and other Windsor pieces

Knell, David *English Country Furniture* (Antique Collector's Club, 2000, orig. 1992) A general guide to English furniture, with a good section on Windsors

Langsner, Drew *The Chairmaker's Workshop* (Lark Books, 1997) A comprehensive book on the methods of making Windsors and ladderback chairs

Massingham, H.J. *Men of Earth* (Chapman & Hall, 1943) Several chapters on traditional Windsor chairmaking

Moser, Thos. *Windsor Chairmaking* (Sterling, 1982) An interesting book concentrating on Thos. Moser's own style of chairs

Nutting, Wallace *Windsor Chairs* (Dover Publications, 2001, orig. 1917) Reprint giving Nutting's personal views on a range of mainly American chairs

Roe, F. Gordon *Windsor Chairs* (Phoenix House, 1953) Excellent overview of Windsors, mainly English

Santore, Charles *The Windsor Style in America* (Courage Books, 1997, orig. 1981) A two-volume book with superb photos of American Windsors

Sparkes, Ivan *English Windsor Chairs* (Shire Publications, 1994, orig. 1981) A booklet on Windsor chairs

Sparkes, Ivan *The English Country Chair* (Spur Books, 1973)

Sparkes, Ivan *The Windsor Chair* (Spur Books, 1975) An overview of the development of Windsor chairs

Sturt, George *The Wheelwright's Shop* (Cambridge University Press, 2000, orig. 1923) Description of Wheelwright's business in the 1880s. The use and choice of wood relevant to Windsor chairs

GLOSSARY

Arbortech Circular blade with chainsaw-type teeth. Fits on to an angle grinder for rapid removal of wood. An alternative to the adze for hollowing seats.

Back-post One of a pair of turned posts that support a crest, with spindles between.

Bending strap Metal strap that supports the outer surface of wood that is being steam-bent, preventing failure. Blocks at either end compress the wood thereby reducing the stretching of the wood in contact with the strap.

Bow/arm Usually steam-bent, but arms are occasionally 'sawn' – made up of three pieces of wood joined together.

Brake Arrangement of posts that allows wood to be held conveniently for splitting, and so that pressure can be applied during splitting to adjust the path of the split through the wood.

Cabinet scraper Piece of sheet metal that can be sharpened with a bur for removing imperfections and smoothing wood.

Drawknife blade with a handle at each end for rapid stock removal, usually of green wood. Always pulled towards the user.

Form/former Pattern (usually made of plywood) for bending wood around, such as arms and bows.

Forstner bit Drill bit that creates a flat-bottomed hole with a small dimple in the centre. These drills will cut overlapping holes without wandering. Ideally used in a drill press.

French polish Shellac dissolved in alcohol.

Green wood Undried wood still containing sap.

Jointing Making a surface flat in preparation for glueing to another flat piece.

Knot Branch of a tree that has been surrounded as the tree grows, causing the surrounding wood to be deformed around it.

Ladderback chair Otherwise known as a 'post and rung' chair. Four vertical posts support the chair and are held together by horizontal rungs. Usually a rush or woven seat.

Medullary rays Ribbons or sheets of material that form perpendicular to the growth rings. These rays are most distinct in species such as oak, and are not obvious in woods such as ash.

Mortice Hole created to accept a tenon.

Pattern maker's vice Versatile vice that can be adjusted to hold irregular-shaped pieces of wood. The jaws can be made non-parallel, they can be rotated, and the whole assembly can be lifted through 90 degrees parallel to the bench.

Ribbon slat Flat strip of wood approximately 1in (2.5cm) wide incorporated on either side of the long spindles in early English Windsor chairs. Usually found in comb-backs, but occasionally found in early double-bow chairs.

Right-angle drill Special drill with the bit held at right-angles to the body, allowing holes to be drilled in confined spaces, such as beneath the arm of a Windsor chair.

Shaving Removing (usually) green wood with a drawknife or spokeshave.

Sight-line Direction of lean of a component such as a leg. The component will lie in a vertical plane above the line.

Spindle Otherwise known as a stick. These elements are found in most Windsor chairs, and are either shaved or turned.

Splat Flat piece of wood incorporated in the centre of the backs of many English Windsor chairs. Earlier splats (eighteenth century) were unpierced, while later splats were inevitably pierced in a decorative pattern.

Spokeshave Either metal or wooden bodied. Wooden shaves have their blade set at a low angle to the wood and are more suitable for Windsor chairmaking. Similar in some ways to a plane, but with a very short sole, and suitable for flat and convex surfaces. Probably the most used tool in Windsor chairmaking.

Stretcher Horizontal element that connects the legs together, adding stiffness and strength to the undercarriage of a chair. The stretcher pushes the legs apart slightly – hence its name.

Tenon Wood shaped to fit into a mortice to make a joint. Can be round or faceted.

Trapping plane Tool designed to create round pieces of varying diameter on a lathe, such as spindles.

Travisher A curved spokeshave designed for hollowing the seats of Windsor chairs after roughing out with an adze.

SUPPLIERS

Cabinetmakers' rasps
www.classichandtools.com

Forstner bits – metric
www.rutlands.co.uk

Forstner bits – imperial
www.fine-tools.com

Auger bits: short, imperial
www.toolbox.co.uk/irwin-marples-r215-short-0-74509

Trapping planes
www.ashemcrafts.com

CAD: Google Sketchup
www.google.com

Froe, adze
www.axminster.co.uk

Abrasives
www.abrasivesplus.com

Milk Paint
www.milkpaint.com

Finishing products
www.restexpress.co.uk

Spokeshaves and travishers
www.thewindsorworkshop.co.uk

ACKNOWLEDGEMENTS

I was lucky to discover my passion for Windsor chairs at the age of thirty-five while taking a course with Jack Hill at West Dean College. That course altered my life! Nancy Goyne Evans' book American Windsor Chairs fuelled my fascination, and to be guided by her around the collection of Windsors at Winterthur was a great privilege.

Mike Dunbar introduced me to green woodworking and techniques to make the chairs that I could picture in my head. Bill Cotton has always been supportive and interested in my work, and I owe him a great debt for letting me study the chair that is the subject of Chapter 8. Michael Harding Hill has encouraged me to make more English chairs and has generously let me study many examples that he owns.

Chloe Darling's enthusiasm for chairs and makers in general has been a great inspiration. Working with her to put on Chairs 2004, and travelling with her to visit Winterthur in 2007, will never be forgotten. Charles Santore's book was, and remains, an invaluable source book for ideas, and it was a great moment to meet him, and to see and discuss his remarkable collection of chairs.

I would like to thank both Eric Gower and Dave Pope for proofreading a draft of this book. Thanks also to Judith Browne for interpreting my rough sketches to create the illustrations. And there are others too numerous to mention who have also encouraged me on this journey. To you all, thank you!

INDEX